JEWISH ENCOUNTERS

Jonathan Rosen, General Editor

Jewish Encounters is a collaboration between Schocken and
Nextbook, a project devoted to the promotion of Jewish literature, culture, and ideas.

>nextbook

PUBLISHED

FORTHCOMING

The Book of Job

HAROLD S. KUSHNER

THE BOOK OF JOB

When Bad Things Happened
to a Good Person

NEXTBOOK · SCHOCKEN · NEW YORK

Grateful acknowledgment is made to the following for permission to reprint previously published material:

HarperCollins Publishers and Michael Katz: Excerpts from
"The Summation" from *The Book of Job*, translated by Stephen
Mitchell. Copyright © 1979 by Stephen Mitchell. Revised edition copyright © 1987 by Stephen Mitchell. Reprinted by permission of HarperCollins Publishers and Michael Katz on behalf
of Stephen Mitchell.

The Jewish Publication Society: Excerpt from "The Book of
Job" appearing in *Tanakh: The Holy Scriptures*. Copyright © 1985
by The Jewish Publication Society. Reprinted by permission of
The Jewish Publication Society.

Library of Congress Cataloging-in-Publication Data
Kushner, Harold S.

The book of Job : when bad things happened to a good
person / Harold S. Kushner.

p. cm.

ISBN 978-0-8052-4292-8

1. Bible. O.T. Job—Commentaries. 2. Suffering—
Religious aspects—Judaism. I. Title.

BS1415.53.K87 2012   223'.106—dc23   2011051531

www.schocken.com

Jacket design by Joey Cofone

Printed in the United States of America

First Edition

2 4 6 8 9 7 5 3 1

CONTENTS

INTRODUCTION

This book represents the closing of a circle. Many years ago, in 1964, I was a young assistant rabbi at a suburban Long Island synagogue and the father of a one-year-old son. I was also pursuing an advanced degree at the Jewish Theological Seminary. I had just passed my oral exams for a doctorate in Bible and met with my adviser, Professor H. L. Ginsberg, chairman of the Bible department, to choose a dissertation topic. He asked me if I had a topic in mind. I told him that I would like to write about the role of God in human tragedy as portrayed in the Bible. As a teenager, I had been shaken when the facts of the Holocaust came to light. Already in my brief career as a rabbi, I had officiated at the funeral of a seventeen-year-old boy who died in a freak accident, I had visited seriously ill congregants in the hospital, I had paid condolence calls on husbands and wives grieving for a life partner taken from them all too soon, and I had felt inadequate when I tried to explain to families why such things happened in God's world. Professor Ginsberg smiled and said, "You're not ready to write that." I ended up writing on the chronology of the biblical psalms.

Over the course of the next dozen or so years, events brought me closer to the issue of life's unfairness and God's role in dealing with it. My wife and I learned that our young son suffered from one of the world's rarest diseases, progeria, the "rapid aging syndrome." He stopped growing and started growing old at age three, and died the day after his fourteenth birthday.

When Aaron was diagnosed with progeria, I read everything I could find about his condition (there was very little available at the time) and everything I could find about God's role in the suffering of innocent children. It was from *Dimensions of Job*, a book edited by Nahum Glatzer and published by Schocken Books, that I drew the ideas that would become the core of my belief system.

After Aaron died, it took two years for me to gain the perspective needed to think about his death in terms of what it meant rather than how much it hurt. I then sat down to write a book about the kind of God I could have faith in and to whom I could turn in a world where good people suffer and die. I called it *When Bad Things Happen to Good People*. It was turned down by two publishers, at which point I took it to Schocken. They liked it, published it, and promoted it. It went on to become a major best seller and a source of comfort to millions.

I would write nine more books to share with my readers the ways in which religion could help them in difficult times. Then two years ago, I was approached by Nextbook, which has been putting out an impressive series of biographies and other books for their Jewish Encounters series in collaboration with Schocken. They asked me to write a book about the biblical book of Job and the question of why good people suffer, a book in which to share the wisdom of the book of Job and its enigmatic answer. This book, then, represents my return to that years-ago conversation with Professor Ginsberg and my return to my first publisher, Schocken Books. It represents my adding my name to the distinguished list of Nextbook authors in their Jewish Encounters series. And it returns me to the issue that I believe I was put on earth to deal with, the question of what kind of world we live in. Is it a world designed to sustain and reward goodness, a world in which God is clearly on the side of the virtuous? Or is it a morally blind world, a morally neutral world in which events happen because they happen, with no deeper meaning? The rain falls equally on the fields of honest and dishonest farmers; malignant tumors afflict charitable and selfish people without distinction. Or is there perhaps a third dimension to our search for meaning, beyond the question of "Why did this happen to me?"

Somewhere, I would like to think, Professor Ginsberg is smiling.

The Book of Job

1

Does Everything Happen for a Reason?

Like many suburban homeowners, my wife and I maintain a bird feeder in our backyard, visible from our kitchen window. We enjoy the songs and the liveliness of the birds, and we feel good about feeding them. But from time to time, for one reason or another—vacations, illness, four inches of snow on the ground—we neglect to refill the feeder. At times like that, I will notice a bird or two come to the feeder looking for food, find none, and fly away. And at times like that, because I am a theologian, I find myself wondering, Do birds wonder why sometimes there is food in the feeder and sometimes the feeder is empty? Do they look for patterns, perhaps making a connection between snow on the ground and an empty feeder? Given that we often make a point of refilling the bird feeder for the Sabbath when we will be at home to enjoy it, do they develop an awareness that every seventh day there will be food for them? Do they ever wonder if something they did was responsible for food being withheld from them?

I can't know for sure, but I suspect that none of the above is true. I suspect that birds come to our backyard, where they have found food before, and if they don't find it, they fly off to look elsewhere. That is one of the differences between human beings and other living creatures. Human beings are meaning-makers, constantly trying to understand our world in terms of cause and effect. We desperately want to believe that the world makes sense, that it is a place where things don't just happen, they happen for a reason. Painful as it may be to conjure with, we want to be told that it was not by accident that a family member got cancer or an earthquake struck a given city, that there was a purpose to it. An unpredictable world, a world of randomness unregulated by cause and effect, would leave us uncomfortable.

Sometimes our insistence on finding patterns of causality in what look like random events can be spectacularly successful. Edward Jenner noticed that milkmaids seemed less vulnerable to smallpox than other people, and fashioned a vaccine that virtually eliminated smallpox. Alexander Fleming noticed that mold in bread kept bacteria in one of his experiments from reproducing, an observation that led to the emergence of penicillin and an array of antibiotics.

Sometimes the impulse to identify cause and effect leads to less desirable results. A farmer's cow gets sick and dies the day after the farmer has had an argument with a neighbor woman. He jumps to the conclusion that the neighbor is a witch who has put a hex on his farm, testifies against her, and would have her hung for witchcraft.

Sometimes the efforts to identify the cause of what has happened can be just plain silly. It has been said that superstitions arise at the intersection of maximum concern and minimum control. We care very much about something—money, love, pregnancy—and if we can't get the result we want by ordinary means, we will resort to all sorts of irrational measures. We see this in matters both vital (serious illness) and trivial (the outcome of a sporting event).

A congregant once told me that when his daughter gave birth to a premature baby, his son-in-law's mother insisted that they hang an amulet on the crib to keep away the evil eye. I asked him if he did it in order to placate her, and he answered indignantly, "Of course not. We're not superstitious people. We didn't hang an amulet; we placed a Bible in the baby's crib instead."

We see this cause-and-effect mentality (the formal name for it in logic classes is *post hoc, ergo propter hoc*, which means "after something, therefore because of that something") in matters large and small. A woman wears her "lucky sweater" to bring her good luck when she plays the slot machines in Las Vegas, because she was wearing it once when she won a significant sum. As the jackpot continues to elude her, she doesn't think, *Slot machines have random payouts and are not affected by what I'm wearing.* She thinks, *I guess I used up the luck in this sweater; I'll have to look for another lucky one.* She is prepared to believe anything to sustain the notion that she has some power over the machine, rather than feel at its mercy.

I know intelligent people, physicians and college professors, who are ardent fans of the Boston Red Sox and believe that things they do or don't do can affect the outcome of a game. One of them continues to blame himself for the Red Sox losing the World Series in 1986. The team was one pitch away from the championship when he left the television set to call his brother to celebrate the win. At that point, everything unraveled and the Sox lost. He insists that as long as he occupied the "power seat" in his den, the Sox prevailed. As soon as he left it, they lost. Clearly, it was his fault.

I'm sure that if I were to say to him, "You're a rational person. You teach philosophy. Do you really believe that where you sit or what you think affects what happens on a baseball field in a different city?" he would answer, "In my rational mind, of course not, but you never know, and when you really care about something, you want to leave no stone unturned. After all, isn't that why seriously ill people, no matter how ruthlessly rational they may be at other times of their lives, go to Lourdes?"

The story is told about the eminent nuclear physicist Niels Bohr that a friend went to visit him in his laboratory and was surprised to see a horseshoe nailed over the entrance. He asked about it and was told that someone had given it to Bohr to bring him luck in his research. The visitor said, "But, Dr. Bohr, you're a scientist. Surely you don't believe in lucky horseshoes!" Bohr answered, "No, of course not. But my friend told me that the wonderful thing about good-luck charms is that they work whether you believe in them or not."

As I said, human beings are meaning-makers. We want to be reassured that we live in a stable, orderly world—that the items we put on our night table when we go to bed will be there in the morning; that they did not fly away or mysteriously disappear. We need to be able to rely on the sun rising in the east every morning and summers being warmer than winters. We search for patterns, and if we search long and hard enough, we find them whether they are really there (texting while driving leads to accidents) or not (lucky sweaters in Las Vegas).

But more than wanting to be reassured that our world is orderly and predictable, we very much want to believe that it is fair, that people get what they deserve. Job's visitors, in the biblical book to which we will shortly turn, struggle mightily not only to find cause for their friend's suffering but to assure themselves that his suffering is morally justified. They would not be comforted if they were told that an all-powerful God inflicted it because He does not care about the moral worth of His victims. And again, the concept of fairness is uniquely human. The Bible describes God, in the opening chapter of Genesis, creating an orderly world, a world in which everything has its place, sky separated from land, land from sea, a world in which every species of plant and animal reproduces after its own kind. Dogs give birth to puppies and no other species, apple trees bear apples and no other fruit. Only with the creation of the first human beings does the orderliness of the world give way to the possibility of unpredictability. Only then can we speak of good and bad rather than convenient and inconvenient. And only then does the question of the world's fairness, its moral as well as its physical reliability, emerge. Will the world reward good people with good outcomes? When a lion kills a zebra, that is not murder, that is dinner, and we never pause to ask ourselves whether the fact that one zebra ran more slowly than the others justified its being killed. But when one human kills another, that is a serious violation of the moral order.

Perhaps no area of life raises more questions about the strength of the moral order of our world than the misfortunes that befall so many of us. A few years ago, a Christian theologian wrote a book-length study of what makes humans unique among all living creatures. He found the crucial difference not in larger brain size, upright posture, opposable thumbs, or the use of language. What makes people unique, he suggested, is our ability to find meaning in suffering. Unlike the birds in our backyard who, when they find the feeding tray empty, fly off to look for food elsewhere, the man or woman who loses a job, is injured in a car crash, or is diagnosed with a malignant tumor feels compelled to ask, "Why? Why did this happen to me and why now?" And if no answer is readily available, he or she will keep searching. Misfortune becomes less painful and more bearable if we can either discern a meaning ("So that is why it happened") or impose a meaning ("What can I do to make something good come out of this?"). Anything is better than the disturbing conclusion that we live in an unfair world, one in which things happen at random.

(A reviewer took issue with the theologian's conclusion. For her, the key to our human uniqueness is our ability not so much to *explain* suffering as to *relieve* it. I think she is on to something.)

For many of us, it is not enough that the world around us be predictable and reliable in natural/geological ways. We want it to be fair, to be as concerned with issues of good and evil as we are. When natural disasters strike, when a hurricane nearly washes away the city of New Orleans, when an earthquake devastates Japan or Haiti, being told that the disaster was caused by warming ocean currents or shifting tectonic plates is not enough of an explanation. We want to know why these people were victims and not some other people, and why at this time and not some other time. We crave reasons, and reasons are never that hard to find if one looks hard enough, especially if the quest involves people we don't know and have never met. So we are told that New Orleans was notorious for corrupt politics and a self-indulgent lifestyle. God sent the hurricane even as He sent a flood to wipe away Sodom and Gomorrah in biblical times. One prominent clergyman sought to explain the earthquake in Haiti by claiming that two hundred years ago, Haitians made a pact with the devil to gain their independence, and this was God's punishment. I would hope that you share my feeling that such "explanations" are not only factually inaccurate but mean-spirited as well, and if they are intended to defend God, they don't work. They leave us with an image of a mean, vindictive deity who may command our fear but does not deserve our worship.

The same desperate quest for reasons comes into play when bad things happen to us and not to someone else, whether a friend or a stranger, and we are tempted to blame ourselves. We tell ourselves, "I must have done something to deserve this," with the second half of the sentence—"because if not, then there is no moral order in the world and I would rather blame myself than believe that"—left unspoken. And typically, few of us have to look very far to find something we did that we could be held accountable for, even if it seems too trivial to justify what happened to us. We are so eager to protect the world's reputation at the cost of our own. I have read of children beaten and abused by alcoholic fathers or mentally ill mothers, who convince themselves that they deserved it and go through life thinking of themselves as having no right to be treated decently because that is preferable to believing that the world is unfair. Such a belief would render our efforts to live righteously pointless. As we will see, Job's response to his suffering will oscillate between insisting that he does not deserve it and pleading, "I can accept this as punishment for something I did if only someone would tell me what it was that I did." At times, it almost seems he would prefer the latter answer. That at least would preserve his sense of the moral order of the universe.

Moreover, accepting blame for the bad things that happen

to us offers another advantage. It makes us feel powerful and dangerous. "My angry thoughts caused my mother's sickness; I am awesomely powerful." "I didn't really want to go on that vacation trip; that's why the accident happened." In 1988, Professor Elaine Pagels wrote *Adam, Eve, and the Serpent* to try to make sense of this tendency of people to blame themselves for things that are clearly not their fault. Why do we do it? Her answer: Many people would rather feel guilty than feel powerless. In a perverse way, it is more comforting to believe "it happened because of me" than to say "I had no impact on what happened."

We want so much to believe that we live in a world that makes sense, a world in which everything happens for a reason, not just natural reasons (it rained because a low pressure area passed over us; my stock portfolio increased in value because of a rise in consumer confidence) but moral reasons (it rained because we are honest, hardworking farmers who prayed for rain; my stocks went up because I turned to God to help me put my child through college and God heard my prayer). And to speak of moral causes for the things that happen is inevitably to invoke God, not just a Creator God who made the world millions of years ago in such a way that rain would fall and crops would grow, but a moral God who rewards goodness and punishes wrongdoing, a God who is a constant, active presence in our world and in our lives.

There is a Jewish legend that describes how Abraham came to believe in God. Unfortunately, the key phrase in the story is just ambiguous enough that it can be interpreted in either of two contradictory ways. The story describes Abraham walking through the desert when he comes upon a palace "lit up by fire." He muses to himself, *Is it possible that no one is in charge of that palace?* At that point, God appears and says to him, I am the master of this palace.

The key phrase is "lit up by fire." What does it mean? Some scholars take those words to mean that there was light throughout the castle, indicating that someone was living there. In an age without electricity, people used fire—candles and torches—to provide light after sunset. The Jewish custom of lighting candles on Friday afternoon to welcome the Sabbath, which we take today as a symbol of peace and serenity, was originally a practical measure to keep people from tripping over the furniture on Friday nights when fires could not be kindled. In this interpretation, the well-lit castle represents a world animated by God's presence. Our world is so well designed that it seems to point to an intelligence behind it. It can't just have happened, any more than a palace could sprout of its own volition in a desert. Someone must have planned it this way. If there was light, someone must live there.

Other scholars interpret the phrase "lit up by fire" to mean that the building was on fire and burning to the ground. Abraham sees it and thinks, *Such a beautiful building. Doesn't anybody live there to take care of it?* At that point, God appears and says to him, Don't be afraid, I am the master of this palace. Bad things may happen in My world. Good things, good people don't last forever. But never suppose that the world has been abandoned and given over to chaos.

One story, two radically different interpretations, two different ways of understanding where to find God's presence.

Interestingly, the Bible, which is the foundation of religious faith in the Western world, does not tell us a great deal about God. There is not a lot of theology in the Hebrew Bible. My teacher Abraham Joshua Heschel used to say that the Bible is not Man's theology but God's anthropology, less about who God is and more about who human beings ought to be. There is a lot about the will of God, what God wants of us, but very little about the nature of God, what we can expect of God, how the mind of God works. What there is can be contradictory. When enemies do harm to Israel, they are sometimes seen as being God's enemies as well, but they are often seen as God's instrument sent to chastise a disobedient people. Sometimes prayer cures illness, and sometimes illness has to run its course despite prayers. How then are we to know whether misfortune is God's doing or an affront to God's will? In the time of Noah, God wipes out virtually the entire population of the earth to punish them for their wickedness. But in the time of Jonah, under very similar circumstances (there are intriguing parallels of language between the two stories), God pardons the wicked inhabitants of the world's largest and most corrupt city when they heed His warning and change their ways.

When we read Homer's *Iliad*, we learn a lot about the Greek gods, their moods, their quarrels, their playing favorites among mortals. We are given reasons why they do the things they do. But reading the Bible, we learn little if anything about God's private life or God's thought processes. Later in their history, Jews would fashion systematic theologies when they lived as a minority among Christians and Muslims and had to explain themselves and their beliefs to their neighbors. But in the Bible itself, theological discourse is rare.

There is one place in the Bible where serious theological conversation about the nature and thought process of God does take place, prompted by the conflict between the human wish to see the world as a moral sphere where people get what they deserve, where everything happens for a reason, and the inescapable reality that ours is a world where good people suffer for no apparent reason. The book of Job is a full-length argument about whether the misfortunes that befall ostensibly good people come to them from the hand of God. If we want to believe that ours is a moral world, the scene of justice and fairness, we need to confront the arguments presented in what is probably the most challenging book in the entire Bible: the book of Job.

2

The Fable of Job

In the Hebrew Bible, the book of Job is found in the third section, known as Ketuvim, (Miscellaneous) Writings, which follows the Torah and the books of the prophets. Ketuvim contains the major books of Psalms, Proverbs, and Job, five smaller "scrolls" (*megillot*) that find their way into the synagogue calendar on various holidays, and several historical books. The three major presences in Ketuvim are sometimes referred to, in an acronym based on their initial letters in Hebrew, as *sifrei emet*, "books of truth," referring to the spiritual truths of the Psalms, the practical truths of Proverbs, and the philosophical-theological insights of Job.

The first thing you need to know about the biblical book of Job is that there are two of them. There is the Fable of Job, a very old, simple folktale of faith maintained and rewarded, found in chapters 1, 2, and 42 of the biblical book. And then there is the Poem of Job, a much later, more complicated work comprising the large middle section of the book. A lot of people reading the Bible don't realize that. They assume it is a single work, a theological sandwich composed of two slices of pious theology wrapped around a dense filling of hard-to-follow religious poetry. The author of the epistle of James in the New Testament didn't know there were two parts to the Job story. He writes, "You have heard of the steadfastness of Job and you have seen the purpose of the Lord, how the Lord is compassionate and merciful" (James 5:11). But the Poem of Job in the Bible shows us a Job who is not necessarily steadfast, who questions the compassion and mercy of God. In fairness to the author of the epistle, his letter is usually dated to late in the first century of the Common Era, and the book of Job may not have been an official part of the Bible at that time, though the Fable seems to have been well-known. The Coen brothers, who in 2009 made the movie *A Serious Man*, a retelling of the story of Job in modern dress, also seem not to have known about the divided nature of the biblical book. Their protagonist, like Job of the Fable but very much unlike Job of the Poem, wonders why bad things keep happening to him but never raises his voice to complain about God. Yet 90 percent of the biblical book of Job portrays a Job who repeatedly challenges the fairness of God. From time to time, a novel or screenplay will be described as "a modern version of the book of Job" when it tells of an innocent person suffering, but the profundity of the biblical book, once we get past the Fable, will be lacking. All of these people are responding to the first two chapters of the biblical book, the Fable of Job, the part of the book that is easiest to understand, and none of them seem to realize that there are forty chapters of sublime and profound protest that come after that and reject the Fable's theology as strenuously as any of these critics do. Even so thoughtful a writer as the late Professor Paul Weiss of Yale, whose book *Right and Wrong* I have read and taught, is moved to write, "The book of Job . . . violates our sense of what is right and wrong." The first two chapters of the book certainly do that, describing a vain God who does not hesitate to inflict suffering on His most devoted followers. The remainder of the book emphatically does not.

Consider some of the major differences between the Fable of Job and the Poem of Job. The Fable is a simple story, in prose, using clear, simple language. The Poem, as you might imagine, is written in poetic form and employs a rich, and often obscure, vocabulary. At one point (4:10–11), the author uses five synonyms for "lion" in the space of two verses. Pity the poor translator. The Fable uses the most sacred Name of God, YHWH, a name that symbolizes God's intimate ties to the Jewish people; the Poem never uses that Name until the very end. It uses less hallowed synonyms—El, Elohim, Shaddai. There are more instances of what is known as a *hapax legomenon*, a word that occurs only once in the Bible so that its meaning may be hard to infer, in the Poem of Job than in virtually any other biblical source. In the Fable, Job is a character; in the Poem, he is the most prominent speaker. But the most important difference is that, in the Fable, Job is never tempted to cry out or express anger toward God. He tells his wife, "Should we accept only good from God and not accept evil?" (2:10), whereas the first thing that Job does in the Poem is to curse the unfairness of his fate. All these factors lead Professor Marvin Pope to write in the Anchor Bible's volume on Job, "Critics have generally regarded the Prologue-Epilogue [what I have called the Fable] and the Dialogue as having diverse authorship and origin." Another scholar puts it this way: "Like oil and water, the prose frame story and the poem tend to disengage from one another despite all efforts to harmonize them."

The Fable, the chapters that Pope refers to as Prologue-Epilogue, tell a simple story. Read chapters 1, 2, and 42 and you will find a coherent, pious fable (with a missing page where thirty-nine chapters of poetry have been inserted). It presents itself at the outset as a "once upon a time" story, with exaggerated virtues, unfathomable suffering, and a happy ending. It resembles stories in the Bible and ancient literature of the good person whose faith is tested but who passes the test with his integrity uncompromised. We think of Joseph spurning the advances of Potiphar's wife (Genesis 39), Daniel refusing to eat forbidden food in the court of King Nebuchadnezzar (Daniel 1), and, most memorably, God commanding Abraham to offer his only son as a sacrifice (Genesis 22).

Once upon a time, the Fable begins, there was a man named Job. The name Job (Iyov in Hebrew) may mean "one whom God treated as an enemy." Or it may just be a name. The man "feared God" and is described as "blameless and upright." He has been blessed by God with abundant wealth (measured by the number of sheep and cattle he owns) and a large family (seven sons and three daughters). The round numbers of sheep, cattle, and children are schematic and mean to signify wholeness. His world is complete, lacking nothing. Not only did Job never sin himself, but when he heard that his sons had been partying, he would offer sacrifices on their behalf the following morning, in case they had gotten carried away in their celebration and done something inappropriate.

Our hero Job is not a Jew, not an Israelite. He is a pious, God-fearing Everyman. In all likelihood, this is an ancient folktale, probably one that circulated in many cultures. A similar story has been found in a Sumerian source dating to approximately 2000 BCE, and another in an ancient Egyptian folktale. Clearly Jews were not the only people who suffered and asked why. Only when an Israelite author appropriated it as the starting point for his inquiry into God's role in human misery did it become Israelite literature and a book of the Bible.

Was Job a real person? Did all those terrible things happen to him and his family? The sages differ. Some, like the twelfth-century commentator Abraham ibn Ezra, insist that he was real, that he was a descendant of Abraham's brother Nahor. Job lived in the land of Uz (pronounced "ootz"), and Uz was the name of Nahor's eldest son. Others, including Maimonides, see the story as a *mashal*, a parable meant to teach us a lesson. It may not be factually, historically true, but it can be true in a more important sense. It can teach us profound truths.

There are multiple links between Job and Abraham beyond the name of Uz. Along with the gentile sailors who are reluctant to throw Jonah overboard in a storm (Jonah 1:16), they are the only men in the Bible described as *y'rei Elohim*, fearing God (Job 1:1, Genesis 22:12; the female midwives in Exodus 1:17 are also so described). As I understand the phrase "fearing God," it has nothing to do with being afraid. It refers to an innate sense of morality, a feeling of horror at the prospect of doing something evil, the perception that some things are so wrong that no one should ever do them. When Abraham, in chapter 20 of Genesis, tries to explain to the king of Gerar why he introduced his wife Sarah as his sister, he explained, "I thought there was no fear of God in this place." He was afraid that the men of Gerar would kill him to take Sarah for themselves. It was not the theology of the Gerarites he was criticizing; it was their lack of decency, their readiness to do something profoundly immoral. Job and Abraham are described as unique for having an innate sense of good and evil that does not depend on revealed law. As we will see shortly, they will share the experience of being "tested" by God when they are asked to deal with the prospect of their children dying.

Though the story of Job does not present itself as a specifically Jewish story, the Fable in the form we have it seems to have been written for a Jewish audience. As noted, the author uses the name YHWH, the personal Name of the

God of Israel, interchangeably with the generic term for divinity, Elohim.

The Fable tells us that one day, Satan appeared before God to report on the doings of God's earthly subjects. God says to Satan, "Have you noticed My servant Job? There is none like him on earth, blameless and upright" (1:8). Satan replies, Well, of course he does good. You have made it worth his while, rewarding him richly for his piety. God insists that Job would be just as faithful even if all those blessings were taken from him. God and Satan enter a wager, to test whether that is indeed the case. Satan sends marauding armies to steal all of Job's cattle and kill his servants. He sends a tornado to destroy the house in which Job's ten children were celebrating, killing them all. (In those days, children were considered an extension of the parent, so that punishing a parent by hurting his child was deemed as acceptable as whipping a person's back to punish him for a crime his hands had committed.) But "despite all that, Job did not sin nor did he cast reproach on God" (1:22).

It is probably impossible for a contemporary reader to read those lines without a significant measure of discomfort. They present a God who plays games with the lives of His creatures to enhance His ego. The narrative calls to mind the line from Shakespeare's *King Lear:* "As flies to wanton boys are we to the gods; they kill us for their sport." Even one of the prominent sages of the Talmud is troubled by God's behavior in the Fable. The Talmud quotes Rabbi Yochanan as saying, "Were it not explicitly written in Scripture, we would not dare say it. God's wager with Satan is like a human being who allows himself to be talked into acting against his better judgment" (Babylonian Talmud, Baba Batra 15a).

We see this troubling motif in one other place in the Bible, in Genesis 22. "Some time afterward, God put Abraham to the test. . . . He said, 'Take your son, your favored son Isaac. Go to the land of Moriah and offer him as a burnt offering' " (Gen. 22:1–2). God's angel intervenes at the last moment to spare the boy, and God tells Abraham, "Because you have done this and have not withheld your son, I will bestow My blessing upon you and make your descendants as numerous as the stars in heaven" (Gen. 22:16–17). The demand to sacrifice Isaac is portrayed as a test, even as the deaths of Job's children are, and the reward for Abraham is the promise of many descendants, as the reward to Job is the blessing of more children. The main difference, no small thing, is that Isaac's life is spared at the end.

What are we to make of that story? How shall we understand God's demand and Abraham's readiness to obey? Throughout the Middle Ages, when Jews were repeatedly victimized and killed by anti-Semitic neighbors, many looked to Abraham as a role model of unflinching loyalty to God and, in some poems written in those times, even presented themselves as superior models of faith because God did not spare their children but they maintained their faith in Him nonetheless.

In modern times, most critics are inclined to see the story

of the near sacrifice of Isaac as an instance of the ancient practice of offering one's firstborn son, along with the first-born of the flocks and the first fruits of the harvest, to God. It was done as a sign of the person's confidence that there would be more blessings from God to replace those that were sacrificed. These critics go on to see God's intervention to spare Isaac's life as ancient Judaism's way of putting an end to the actual sacrificing of children, though the custom remained in Israel of dedicating one's firstborn son to assist in the sanctuary. See the story of the birth of Samuel in chapter 1 of the first book of Samuel, and the rite of *pidyon ha-ben*, "redeeming" one's firstborn son from a Kohen, a representative of the Temple of olden days. Well into the twentieth century, many Roman Catholic families felt an obligation to send at least one of their sons into the priesthood.

In more recent times, some highly imaginative interpretations of God's demand that Abraham sacrifice his child have been offered. Some years ago, a physician suggested that Isaac was a child with severe developmental issues. He is born to elderly parents, he is often a strangely passive person, and he is the only man in the entire Bible whose parents have to arrange a marriage for him. The doctor suggested that when Abraham heard God's command that he put Isaac to death on an altar, what he was hearing was his own ambivalence about having to raise a special-needs child.

One particularly intriguing theory, one to which I find myself drawn, was put forth a while back by Freud's disciple Theodore Reik in his 1961 book, *The Temptation*. Reik sees the story as originally having described a coming-of-age ritual like the ones found in many Near Eastern and African societies, where a boy on the threshold of puberty is taken away from his mother and other women, asked to undergo a life-threatening experience, sometimes even mimicking death, representing the end of childhood and his entry into adult status. (Think of it as Isaac's bar mitzvah.) When he survives, the lore of the tribe is disclosed to him and he is recognized as a man. Only later, Reik suggests, was it recast as a story in which Isaac's life was actually in danger, possibly as a step toward the elimination of child sacrifice.

Then, in 2009, an American-born Israeli scholar, Judy Klitsner, wrote a fascinating book, *Subversive Sequels in the Bible*. Her thesis is that sometimes the editors of the Bible, entrusted with putting into words the divine revelation, were troubled by a nuance of an ancient story as it had been passed down. Unable to change the original source, they would tweak a later story to offer a more acceptable message, linking the two stories by the repetition of key words so that alert readers would get the point. Klitsner notes linguistic echoes of Job in the story of Abraham and Isaac. (If the tradition is to be credited, Job lived after the time of Abraham, but it is highly likely that the Fable was in circulation while the narrative of Genesis was still being polished.) After God intervenes to spare Isaac's life, He praises Abraham as *y'rei Elohim*, one who fears God, the same phrase used to describe Job. Both Job (42:6) and Abraham (Gen. 18:27) describe themselves as "dust and ashes" when they confront

God, and both come to the end of their lives "old and contented" (Job in 42:17; Abraham in Genesis 25:8). Following Klitsner's theory of a "subversive sequel," might we suspect that the narrative of the Akedah, the near sacrifice of Isaac, was phrased in part as a curative for people of faith who were appalled at God's treatment of Job's children? It would say to the reader (back then, more likely the listener), Don't be upset by that old notion of God. God as we have come to know Him will not let the child die.

The concept of a God who learns from His mistakes is not unknown in Jewish lore. A familiar midrash describes God as first creating a world dominated by the standard of strict justice, but it could not last. People could not be that perfect. God then tries a world run by forgiveness, but finds that that too cannot be sustained. Finally He created the world as we know it. The boldest statement I know of along those lines comes from *The Personhood of God* by the late Professor Yochanan Muffs of the Jewish Theological Seminary. Not specifically referring to either Job or Abraham, Muffs writes, "God was a king who in His youth behaved in one way, and in His older age, poetically speaking, in yet another. Having learned from His mistakes, He now allows His mercy to override His anger."

We now return to the Fable of Job. God now turns to Satan and says, Have you noticed that Job has not been shaken in his faith, despite what you persuaded Me to do to him? Doesn't that prove that he is a man of total integrity? Satan counters, It doesn't prove a thing. You've only taken his property, which can be replaced. Touch him personally and see how quickly he will turn against You. So God afflicts Job with a disease over all of his body, causing him constant pain. His wife urges him to curse God and be struck dead for it, to be put out of his misery, but he rebukes her. Three friends come to console him in his bereavement and his illness. Before they can say anything, the tone of the narrative changes from prose to poetry, and Job's quiet acceptance of God's punishment changes to soaring rage against it. One senses that there was originally a page in which the friends, like Job's wife, tell him that God does not deserve his loyalty if God can treat him like this, and Job rebukes them as well.

In chapter 42, beginning with verse 7, we find the conclusion, the happy ending of the Fable. God appears and chastises the friends for having spoken falsely about Him. Job, ever the pious one, intercedes on his friends' behalf. God then restores Job's fortune, with more sheep and cattle, and new children to replace the ones who died. A student once asked me if the same wife who gave birth to Job's first ten children many years earlier also gave birth to these ten. I think the appropriate question (remember, this *is* only a story) would not be about the burden imposed on the wife by ten late-in-life pregnancies, but about the notion that children who die can be replaced by other children. As a father who has lost a child, I can testify that the answer to that question is both yes and no. There is comfort in seeing the empty space filled by another child, by a son-in-law, by a grandchild. But the emptiness, the sense that "there should be someone else there," remains. There is a rabbinic proverb, "When you dig a pit, there is never enough earth to refill it." In the world of real holes dug in the ground, that is manifestly not true. There is always dirt left over. We can never pack it in as densely as we found it. But if we take the pit to be a reference to the grave, then it is true. We can fill the emptiness, but a measure of emptiness remains. Jacob in the Bible has a houseful of children and grandchildren, yet he never gets over the (presumed) death of Joseph.

Job's relatives and friends come to console him for his losses, each of them bringing him a small gift, and there are so many of them that he is left even wealthier than he was before. (The text is not clear as to whether these gifts were in addition to God's restoring Job's fortune, or whether this was how it happened.) His steadfast piety has been rewarded, and Job dies old and contented.

That is the ancient folktale, the Fable of Job, as told to countless people over the course of generations to encourage them to be steadfast in their faith no matter what happens to them. It probably comforted many people in olden days, but for the contemporary reader, it may leave us with more questions than answers. Perhaps the first set of questions would have to do with Satan: Who is he, what is his relationship to God, and why is he out to get Job?

First of all, the Satan of chapter 1 in Job is not the Satan of Milton's *Paradise Lost*, the fallen angel, prince of darkness, and enemy of God, who proclaims, "Evil, be thou my good."

Neither is he the Mephistopheles of Goethe's *Faust*, the agent of temptation and damnation. He is not the Satan who tempts Jesus in chapter 4 of the gospel of Luke and in Matthew as well. That Satan offers earthly rewards for prideful behavior. Satan in the Fable deals in punishment, not prizes. And he is certainly not the red-tinted figure with horns and a pitchfork whom we find in so many cartoons of Hell. This Satan works for God and is powerless to do anything without God's approval.

Who is he and why does he cast aspersions on God's followers? Some scholars connect the name Satan to a Hebrew verb meaning "to obstruct or impede." They translate the Hebrew, which always carries the definite article "the" (Satan is a title, a job description, not a name), as the Tempter (influenced perhaps by the passage from Luke), the Adversary, or the Accuser. Goethe calls him "the spirit of negation," the one who doubts everything and sees only the worst in people. The word "satan" is used metaphorically in Psalm 109, verse 6, where the psalmist wishes that his enemy be summoned to court with an accuser (a satan) across from him. Satan appears in the Hebrew Bible there and in Zechariah 3:1–2, where he seeks to persuade God that Joshua is unfit to serve as high priest in the restored Temple of Jerusalem, and God rebukes him and affirms Joshua's fitness. Then there is a strange passage in I Chronicles 21:1. It tells of how "Satan arose against Israel and incited David to number Israel"—that is, to conduct a census. This was considered a taboo in the ancient world, a harbinger of misfortune, like the parent who brags of how many children he has, only to have misfortune strike one of them. (Taking a census may have gotten a bad reputation because it was often followed by a tax increase or a military draft.) God strikes Israel with a plague, which ends only when David repents and begs God to forgive him. Significantly, the parallel passage in 2 Samuel 24:1 speaks of *God* inciting David to do wrong, not Satan.

"Satan" also occurs as a verb in Numbers 22:22. The gentile wizard Balaam has been hired by the king of Moab to curse Israel, and Balaam accepts the commission even though God has told him not to go. He sets out in defiance of God, and God sends an angel "to be a Satan against him," to block his way and keep him from going. Translations I consulted render that verbal phrase as "impede," "obstruct," or "be an adversary." This angel, like Satan in the Fable, is God's agent, but unlike the figure in the Fable, the angel in Numbers 22 does not merely report; he acts. The best explanation I know of is the theory of the Israeli scholar N. H. Tur-Sinai. He derives the name Satan from the Hebrew root *shoot/shattat*, meaning "to roam, to go back and forth," and sees his role as that of "God's spy" who would go around the world checking on people's activities and eavesdropping on their conversations to report any trace of disloyalty to God. Notice that when the Satan first appears in the story of Job, God asks him, "Where have you been?" and he replies, "I have been roaming [in Hebrew, *shoot*] all over the world." The historian Herodotus writes of men known as "the eyes and ears of the king," sent out by the kings of Persia to ferret out disloyalty.

They would sit in the marketplaces and listen for complaints about taxes or the criticizing of government officials, and report them to the king. The Greek translations of the Bible use the word "diabolos," informer, for Satan, from which we get the English words "devil" and "diabolical."

Satan, then, can be seen as God's spy. We gather that he shows up regularly when God holds court with a list of people who have been cheating on their wives, overcharging their customers, and scoffing at God. On the day described in chapter 1, when all the members of the divine court including Satan assemble in God's presence, God challenges Satan, Enough bad news. Have you considered my servant Job? He never does anything wrong or disloyal. It is at that point that Satan challenges God to test Job's faith.

It is interesting to note that Job's wife, who is more of a prop than a real person in the story, seems to share Satan's view of human nature. For her as for him, it makes sense for a person to be pious and loyal to God only if that leads to a rich and happy life. Take away the rewards of piety and it's not worth it. I have had congregants like that, such as the man who said to me, "If this could happen to my family, what was the point of our being observant and coming to synagogue all those years?" I have an answer to that question, but at that point he was probably not in a mood to hear it. Where Satan says to God, The only reason Job is faithful is because You reward him for it, Job's wife tells her afflicted husband, If something like this can happen to you, what was the point of being so pious? Curse God, let Him strike you dead, and you'll be put out of your misery. Job answers her, "You speak like a foolish woman. Shall we accept the good from God and not the ill?" (2:10). With those words, Job proves Satan wrong. He is steadfast in his faith even when everything he had has been taken from him. But at the same time, he acknowledges God as the source of his suffering and, at least by implication, concedes that there is no necessary link between how people live and what happens to them. Job may be moral and righteous, but the God of the Fable is not. For the twenty-five hundred years that separate the book of Job from our own time, Jewish theology has ranged between two poles, the certainty that God knows what He is doing and our refusal to believe that our misfortune could possibly be the will of a righteous God.

That should be the end of the story, and once upon a time, it probably was. Three friends make an appearance, a condolence call on their friend whose children have died, and we can assume that, in the course of their remarks, they too bemoan the unfairness of life and how badly God treats His most loyal followers. And presumably Job refutes them as well.

Then, in the happy ending preserved in chapter 42, verses 7–17, God appears, praises Job for his loyalty, rebukes the friends for the shallowness of their devotion, and restores Job's fortunes.

That is the Fable. After reading it, we have come to know Job. He is a man of unshakable faith in God no matter what life deals him. We have come to understand Job's wife and his friends who question the point of living righteously if God treats us all arbitrarily. We even understand Satan, whose job description leads him to be cynical about the most ostensibly virtuous of men. But what does the Fable of Job teach us about God?

The God of the Fable is a God who prizes unquestioning loyalty and absence of criticism over all other virtues. One serves God with good deeds but also with gifts of animal offerings to atone for misbehavior. God is all-powerful and all-controlling (but not necessarily all-knowing; He apparently needs to employ "spies"). Everything that happens in the world is an expression of His will. But He is not a moral being in the sense that we have come to understand the term. He does things that would seem petty and sinful if done by humans—killing people for no cause, inflicting illness on the innocent, and brooking no criticism ("challenge God and die").

Perhaps in an age of despotic kings and rulers, people had to believe in a God who was at least as powerful as an earthly king. If the king had arbitrary power over life, death, and property, how could people take seriously a God who could do less?

Or perhaps people had no trouble believing in and worshipping a God like that because it answered the question we posed in the previous chapter, Does everything happen for a reason? It may be that people felt more reassured by positing a world totally controlled by an all-powerful but arbitrary

God than by believing in an arbitrary world ruled by a God who did not always control what happened in it. "God must have His reasons" is more comforting than "some things happen for no reason and there is nothing God can do about it." Maybe our need to believe that "somebody is in charge" is so strong that we can overlook flaws in God that we would condemn in anyone else.

But where does that theology leave us? We can *fear* a God who is above moral considerations that set limits on His freedom to act, but can we *love* such a God? Fear tends to drive out love as surely as love drives out fear. Can we turn to such a God for strength and solace when bad things happen to us, if those bad things are seen as God's will? Can we work to cure diseases and undo the damage of hurricanes without feeling that we are acting against God, if the diseases and hurricanes are seen as God's doing? And where does our sense of morality come from in the first place, the instinct that even young children have, to feel that certain things are unfair? From where do we learn not to abuse the poor or take advantage of the vulnerable if those directions do not come from God, if God Himself is immune to such "soft" considerations? It is like the folk proverb "If you see a blind man, kick him; why should you be kinder than God?"

If you were bothered by such considerations as you read the Fable of Job, if you find its view of God less reassuring and more troubling than people of long ago did, you are not alone nor are you the first to feel that way. Some twenty-five centuries ago, a writer blessed with a mind of great subtlety and a vocabulary unmatched by any other biblical author had the same reaction. He took the venerable, pious Fable of Job, turned it inside out, and gave us the theological masterpiece we know as the book of Job in the Bible.

3

The Poem of Job

Once you get past the first two chapters, the book of Job is perhaps the most challenging book to understand in all the Bible. It is probably impossible to understand it fully. But it is worth the effort. The Poem of Job is one of the most sublime creations in all of biblical literature—in fact, in all of literature. Tennyson, who knew something about poetry, called it "the greatest poem of ancient and modern times." Thomas Carlyle said of it, "There is nothing written in the Bible or out of it of equal literary merit." There are at least three reasons for its being a hard work to understand.

The first is the language. As mentioned earlier, Job uses more words that occur nowhere else in the Bible than virtually any other book. Because many of them seem related to similar words in Aramaic (a language related to Hebrew and spoken by more people than Hebrew in ancient times; it would later be the language spoken by Jesus and by Jews in the first centuries of the Common Era), several reputable scholars believe that the book of Job was originally written in Aramaic and then translated into Hebrew. I find their argument unpersuasive for two reasons. First, the poetry of Job reaches such sublime heights that it is hard to believe that we are not reading it in its original language. In addition, if someone translated the book from an Aramaic original, why didn't he translate it into familiar Hebrew words rather than obscure Aramaisms? Isn't that the whole point of a translation?

In addition to vocabulary issues, the subtlety of language often leaves us wondering just what a phrase means, even when we think we understand the words. Does Job say in 19:25, "I know that my Redeemer lives," or is he saying, "I would rather be redeemed while I'm still alive"? The latter fits the Hebrew better, but the former is more congenial to Christian theology. Again, in 13:15, is he saying, "Though He slay me, yet will I trust in Him," or "He may slay me, I have no hope"? In each case, either translation fits the Hebrew text as we have it, and the choice often seems to depend on the theology of the translator. The temptation for many a Bible scholar is to assume that the genius who wrote the book believed and thought much as the scholar does. The text becomes a mirror in which we see our own face reflected. And some verses simply defy translation. The Septuagint, the translation of the Hebrew Bible into Greek under Jewish auspices, leaves out several dozen verses of Job, presumably because the translators despaired of making sense of them. In the English translation of Job that I use, virtually every page has a footnote that reads "meaning of Hebrew uncertain."

A second barrier to understanding the book is its subject matter. The issue of the nature of God and God's relationship to events on earth is about as profound as it gets. Imagine trying to read a book that combines the complexity of a college philosophy text with the poetic language and imagery of a Shakespearean tragedy, and you get a sense of the challenge that the Poem of Job represents.

And finally, our efforts to understand the poem are complicated still further by the fate of the text itself. It is almost certain that the book as we have it is not identical to the one the author wrote. In an age before printing presses, manuscripts were copied by hand, often by scribes who could not understand or might be offended by the words in front of them. Slips of the pen, the human equivalent of typographical errors, and misreading Hebrew letters that look similar, inevitably occurred. A scribe's eye might slip from one line to a similar word in the line below and an entire sentence could be lost. Thus we find hundreds of discrepancies, usually minor, between the biblical text as we have it and the fragments of the text found among the Dead Sea Scrolls.

Moreover, if the scribe should encounter a passage whose content troubled him, he might take it upon himself to change the text in front of him, either because he believed a pious author could not have intended to write such a sentence or because he feared the author meant it and the scribe was reluctant to promote false ideas. We have an example of this in chapter 2 of the second book of Samuel. King Saul has died in battle against the Philistines, and there is a vacancy in the position of king of Israel. The southern tribes choose David to be their king in Saul's place while the northern tribes prefer to follow Saul's son, whose name is given as Ish-Boshet. That was certainly not his real name. Ish-Boshet means "man of shame." What parent, and especially what king, would give his son a name like that? We know from a parallel passage in the first book of Chronicles (8:33) that his real name was Ishbaal, which means "man of Baal." Baal was the name of the Canaanite god of power. King Saul probably did not believe in or worship Baal, any more than Jewish parents who name their daughter Natalie (derived from Natal, December 25, the birthday of Jesus) are making a theological statement, but he may have thought that the name conveyed strength and manliness. Whatever the reason, it would seem that a pious scribe, copying the text of Samuel, was embarrassed to attach the name of Baal to an Israelite prince and changed it to "man of shame." In the same way, I can picture a pious scribe being so offended by some of the arguments in the Poem of Job that he either altered the text to make it less heretical or even left lines out entirely. I remember a Bible class I had as a teenager, in which we were studying Ecclesiastes, another challenging book. Our teacher, an Orthodox Jew, gave us a list of verses we were to read for homework and another list of verses he told us to skip because of their heretical implications. You can guess which ones we read first. And as we will see when we come to chapter 32 of the poem, some scribes may not have been above adding their own messages where they felt the author did not make the case for God strongly enough.

Does it shock you to be told that a copyist might have taken liberties with the text he was paid to copy? It probably happened less when it came to copying the Torah, which was seen as God's word, than it did with the wisdom literature. But the notion of the inviolability of a text is more recent than you might assume. It has been suggested that, when a book was written anonymously, as Job was, a scribe may have felt, consciously or unconsciously, that it was "public property," open for him to improve on. In seventeenth-century England and nineteenth-century America, producers of Shakespeare's plays felt free to eliminate scenes to shorten the play, drop some characters to save on production costs, and even change the endings of tragedies to happy outcomes. Copyright laws would come later.

But the effort to understand the Poem of Job is well worth it. The problems I cited raise the question of how we read a book, and the answer depends on its nature and subject matter. We read some books for plot. Thrillers, detective mysteries, romantic novels are written primarily to divert and entertain us. When I was younger, they tended to be longer, with longer chapters, and were thought of as "beach reading." Today they tend to have shorter chapters and seem to have been written for reading on airplanes. I once delayed getting off a transcontinental flight until I assured myself that the completely fictional hero of the book I was reading would escape safely from a completely imaginary predicament. Graham Greene, late in his career, would not even classify some of his short works of fiction as novels, calling them instead "entertainments."

Some books invite us to savor the thoughtful use of language and development of character. At their best, they leave us with memories of personalities against which we measure ourselves and people in our own lives. They deserve to be read more slowly. My own rule of thumb is to read a book as slowly and carefully as it seems to have been written. If I sense that the author labored to come up with just the right word or metaphor, I try to read it carefully enough to appreciate the effort.

Some books are written to be useful. As a writer, I was dismayed recently to read that something like 70 percent of novels are written by women to be read by other women, and 70 percent of nontextbook nonfiction books are books about succeeding in business, written by men to be read by men.

And then there are books that are meant not just to divert us or enhance our earning capacity but to change us as we read them. They want us to respond by thinking not just *This is a good story* or *This is useful for me to know*, but *This is my story the author is writing about. This is an issue I've been bothered by for a long time; let me see what he has to say about it.*

The Poem of Job is that kind of book. It asks questions like Do we live in a world that rewards people for being honest and charitable?, and if so, in what currency does that reward arrive? Does God care about what kind of person I am? Can a religious person be angry at God, even doubt the existence of God, and still think of himself or herself as a religious person? The Poem of Job does not have an answer to those questions; it has answers. It invites us to look at the world through the eyes of several characters, some who challenge God, some who defend God, and ultimately from the viewpoint of God Himself. It is an extraordinary experience to be changed by a book as we read it, to see the world differently because of it, and the Poem of Job strives to be that kind of book. I will do my best to guide you through the linguistic and theological challenges that fill the book, and I will ask you to imagine yourself into the mind-set of each of the characters as we read their words together.

The author of the Poem totally leaves the Fable behind. There are no more references to God's wager with Satan, and he feels no need to justify a God who kills innocent people to win a bet. Instead, there is a no-holds-barred argument about God's role in the world, the likes of which we find nowhere else in the Bible.

Too many readers are inclined to dismiss the Fable as simpleminded and then dismiss the Poem as too complicated to understand. I will not try to explain every verse of the Poem. There are any number of very good commentaries that do that, and from time to time I will cite them. Instead, I will focus on what I deem to be the key verses in every chapter, translating their poetry into accessible prose and their often elusive theology into terms the average reader will be able to understand. Unless otherwise attributed, all extended citations of text are taken from the Jewish Publication Society's 1980 translation. I will also be drawing on the insights of several scholars, notably Marvin Pope in his commentary for the Anchor Bible series, Robert Gordis (who was my teacher) in *The Book of God and Man*, Carol Newsom of Emory University in *The Book of Job*, and the gifted literary critic Robert Alter in his recent commentary, *The Wisdom Books*.

Some scholars insist on defending the unity of the book. There are examples in antiquity of prose introductions to poetic works, and Shakespeare does it in *As You Like It*. Why, they ask, couldn't a skilled author use a prose prologue, maybe a familiar story, to set the stage for a longer, more nuanced discussion of the question of God and evil? It is certainly possible, but I don't think that argument is true to the nature of the book. Job in the Poem not only speaks in different rhythms than Job of the Fable, poetry rather than prose; he is an entirely different person, no longer meekly accepting the evil from God as readily as he gratefully accepts the good. This Job is angry at God, challenging God, complaining about God's unfairness. And if the Fable, despite its old-fashioned diction and point of view, comes from the same hand as the Poem, why at the end, when God finally deigns to answer Job, are there no references to Satan or to the wager? To me, it makes far more sense to read the Poem as a challenge to, and a rejection of, the theology of the Fable.

If we grant that the Fable was an old, familiar folktale whose origins are lost in the mists of time, when might the

Poem of Job have been written? I wrote my doctoral dissertation (after Professor Ginsberg persuaded me not to try to write on Job) on the question of when the biblical psalms might have been composed, and the first challenge I had to confront was the difficulty of dating a poem in which there are no historical points of reference. When Psalm 137 speaks of sitting by the waters of Babylon and weeping for the destroyed Temple of Jerusalem, we can say with some confidence that it was written shortly after the destruction of the Temple in 586 BCE. But when the Twenty-third Psalm speaks of finding God in the valley of the shadow of death, how can we even guess as to when that encounter might have taken place? Job fits the latter example more closely than the former. In addition, in trying to guess its date of origin, we have to beware the temptation to say that because something shows great sophistication and depth, it must have come later rather than earlier. Among nineteenth- and twentieth-century Bible critics, this manifested itself in a blatant pro-Christian bias: David, that bloodthirsty adulterer, could not have written the Psalms; such sublime prayers must have been composed closer to the time of Jesus. If Job is the most profound, most intellectually challenging book in the Bible, for such critics it was irresistible to see it as coming at the end of a long period of theological thinking. But are we just displaying our own biases when we think that way?

There is one date that serves as a dividing line, cleaving biblical literature into "before" and "after." The year is 586 BCE, when the Babylonians destroyed the Temple and sent the people of Judea into exile. Before that, the Israelites were a nation in their own land, with their own king. Afterward, they were a minority in the several lands of their dispersion (as in the books of Daniel and Esther) or, after the Return, a province in someone else's empire (as in the books of Ezra and Nehemiah and several of the so-called minor prophets). We would expect religious compositions to betray the circumstances of their origin along those lines. But that is of limited help in determining the date of composition of Job. Some critics insist that it must be relatively early, pre-exilic. How can someone write about God's letting good people suffer after the fall of the Temple and not allude to that event? Others say that that is the best argument for a late date, by which time the Israelites were all too experienced with the subject of good people suffering. We also note that, at a number of points, passages in Job are strikingly similar to passages in Jeremiah and the Psalms. Can we infer that the author may have lived late enough to be familiar with those works? Or are those only examples of parallel inspiration, creative minds responding in similar ways to similar provocations? The only conclusion we can come to with any certainty is that we don't know, we will probably never know, and it really doesn't make that much difference. People like Job have lived in every century, in every generation, and we who observe them have been stirred in every age to ask, Why?

If the date of the book's origin is irretrievable, if the language is often a challenge, at least the structure of the book is admirably clear. Beginning with chapter 3, when the book shifts from prose to poetry and Job evolves from patient to angry, Job speaks at length. Then Eliphaz, one of three friends who have come to comfort him, offers another point of view, challenging what Job has said, and Job responds to him. After that, Bildad, a second visitor, speaks to Job and Job answers him. Job's third guest, Zophar, gets his turn and hears Job's rejoinder as well. That ends the first cycle.

There follows a second cycle with tempers growing steadily shorter, each of the friends' remarks followed by Job's response, and the beginnings of a third, which degenerates into total textual confusion, either by design of the author, to show us the participants losing patience with each other, shouting and interrupting one another, or because some anonymous scribe, deliberately or due to limited competence, rearranged some of the text. That sets the stage for the unforgettable, if enigmatic, conclusion of the book.

Although the arguments of the four participants will at times require close reading and some intelligent guesswork, what they are arguing about is clear enough. Job challenges the fairness and kindness of God, and the friends defend God. You may remember the "eternal triangle" of college discussions about God's goodness. We would begin with three statements, only two of which can be true:

> God is all-powerful.
> God is completely good.
> Evil exists.

The challenge to the believer in God is to harmonize all three or, if he cannot, to suggest which one has to be sacrificed to sustain the other two. Either there are some things God cannot do, or it does not bother God to permit evil, or what seems evil to us is really not evil if we knew all the facts.

The discussion in Job roughly follows that structure, with one important change. The three statements all participants seek to maintain are these:

> God is all-powerful.
> God is completely good.
> Job is a good person.

Since it is logically impossible for a completely good God to let an innocent man like Job suffer if He could prevent it, one of those three statements must be false. Which one? That is what the book of Job will spend the next twenty-five chapters talking about. Job's three visitors will challenge assumption number three, that Job is a good person. If he were, why would God let this happen to him (unless, perhaps, as a warning)? Job will affirm God's power but challenge His uncompromised goodness. He is so powerful that no rules of conventional morality bind Him. Opinions will evolve and sharpen, building to an unforgettable conclusion. It is to that theological debate, one that has no parallel in the Bible or in ancient literature, that we now turn.

4

The Argument Begins

Before we examine the first cycle of speeches, comprising chapters 3–14 of the biblical book, there are a few things we should keep in mind. First, Job's friends have not come to his home to argue with him or to refine his theology. Their friend has suffered bereavement and illness, and they genuinely want to make him feel better. They have come to say things to Job that they are sure he will find comforting, things they would find comforting were they in his place.

Second, Job is not looking for vindication. At the outset he does not protest his innocence. He knows that, as a fallible human being, he is not perfect. He concedes that his punishment has come at the hands of a righteous God. What he wants is for God, or someone, to make sense of his punishment, to tell him what he has done to deserve such misery. Without knowing that, how can he repent and improve? Job does not want to believe that God makes mistakes, that He sometimes punishes the wrong people. Job *wants* to be proven wrong and deserving of punishment, to reassure him that God knows what He is doing. To be told that he is sinless and is suffering for no reason would shake his faith in God's rule over the world.

I am reminded of an incident in my own life some years ago. We received a letter from our bank telling us that our checking account was overdrawn. I checked our record book, which showed that we had a balance of well over a thousand dollars. I went down to the bank, indignantly, to challenge them, to say to them, We don't write checks for money we don't have. It turned out the bank was right and I was wrong. Two weeks earlier, I had planned to go to the bank during my lunch hour and deposit my monthly paycheck. Anticipating that, I entered the deposit in my record book. But an emergency came up in the congregation, and I never had lunch, nor did I visit the bank that afternoon. I finally deposited my check two days later and entered the deposit a second time. Not surprisingly, the bank counted it only once. But what I remember most clearly about that incident was neither my embarrassment at having made that mistake nor my chagrin at having less money than I thought I had. What I remember is a sense of relief. I was relieved to know that the bank keeps accurate records and that we did not have to rely on my sometimes shaky mathematical skills to know where we stood.

That is Job's attitude when the discussion begins. To be told that he is in fact innocent (as the Fable portrays him) and that God punishes people who don't deserve to be punished would not bolster his faith in himself as much as it would shake his faith in God.

Before we turn to the text of the Poem, I would call your attention to something the four participants in the conversation do, perhaps because they are fictional characters. They actually listen to each other, rather than spending the moments when someone else is speaking thinking about what they will say next. Their positions change and evolve as a result of what the previous speaker has said. And as many critics have pointed out, it is to the anonymous author's credit that he grants equal depth and eloquence to all participants, though his sympathies are clearly with Job.

With those thoughts in mind, we turn to the text.

Job's Outburst: Chapter 3

In accordance with the custom followed by observant Jews to this day, Job's comforters sit quietly until Job breaks the silence in an outburst of pain and grief.

> Perish the day on which I was born,
> And the night it was announced, A male child has
> been conceived.
> May that day be darkness, May God have no concern
> for it
> May light not shine on it . . .
> Why did I not die at birth,
> Expire as I came out of the womb?

Why were there knees to receive me, breasts for me to
     suck?
For now I would be lying in repose, asleep and at rest,
With the world's kings and counselors who rebuild
     ruins for themselves . . .
There the wicked cease from troubling,
There rest those whose strength is spent . . .
Small and great alike are there,
And the slave is free of his master. (Job 3:2–4, 11–14,
     17, 19)

There is a theory put forth by some child psychologists
that speech is born of frustration. If an infant could arrange
to be fed and changed merely by needing it, if he could get
everything he wanted just by wanting it, he would never
learn to speak. (It's like the old joke about the boy who
never talked. His parents took him to doctors and specialists
and they could never find anything wrong with him, but he
never said a word. Then one morning at breakfast, he looked
up and said, "My oatmeal's cold." The parents were ecstatic.
He could talk, he was normal. They asked him, "Why did
you never speak before this?" He answered, "The oatmeal
was always fine till now.") Job breaks his weeklong silence
during the friends' condolence call not to ask for anything
or to share any thoughts but simply to give voice to his pain
and anguish. He is saying, passionately and eloquently, *I wish
I were dead. In fact, I wish I had never been born or that I had died
at birth. All the good things of my life till now were not worth it*

if they end in such unbearable pain. If he were dead, he would be the equal of kings and rulers, at rest in their graves and immune to pain and pleasure alike. The reference to building ruins may refer to monuments like the pyramids of Egypt or to elaborate palaces that deteriorated after the death of their builders. I like the Anchor Bible's rendering of Job's first line, "Damn the day I was born." "Perish" is closer to the Hebrew, but "damn" catches the mood and the rhythm of Job's outburst better.

The passage is strikingly similar to Jeremiah 20:14–17. There the prophet has been beaten and imprisoned for warning the people that they do not deserve God's protection in the coming war, and he complains to God about the burden of being a prophet in these words: "Accursed be the day that I was born . . . accursed be the man who brought my father the news . . . and gave him such joy. . . . Why did I ever issue from the womb?" One wonders if the author of Job was familiar with that passage.

Notice that there is no theology in Job's lament. He never asks, Why is God doing this to me? Where is God when I need Him? The only reference to God in the entire speech is an indirect one: "Why does He give light to the sufferer and life to the bitter in spirit?" (3:20).

The friends are sensitive enough to listen patiently to Job's lament and not try to talk him out of his feelings. They are not bad people, nor are they looking for a theological disputation. In the beginning, at least, they do not take issue with anything Job says. They offer what they believe are words of comfort, words they have probably spoken dozens of times to friends and neighbors in similar circumstances, words that Job himself has probably spoken to others. And it is they who first invoke the name, and the involvement, of God.

Eliphaz Tries to Comfort Job: Chapters 4–5

Eliphaz, who seems to be the most senior and the most thoughtful of the three visitors, speaks first. He makes two points, beginning by reminding Job of how he has counseled others:

> See, you have encouraged many, You have
>   strengthened failing hands.
> Your words have kept him who stumbled from falling,
> You have braced knees that gave way.
> But now that it overtakes you, it is too much. (4:3–5)

Eliphaz is asking Job, What would you say to someone in your situation? In fact, what *have* you said to such a person so often? Say it now to yourself.

> Is not your piety your confidence, Your integrity your
>   hope?
> Think now, what innocent man ever perished?

Where have the upright been destroyed?
As I have seen, those who plan evil and sow mischief
    reap them.
They perish by a blast from God. (4:6–9)

How can Eliphaz see his friend Job bereaved, afflicted, and
say to him "What innocent man ever perished?" It strikes
the reader as grossly insensitive, unless we understand Eliphaz to be saying, Job, we are in the middle of your story,
not at its end. You have to believe that God "who performs
great deeds that cannot be fathomed . . . who gives rain to
the earth, who raises the lowly up high [and] saves the needy
from the clutches of the strong" (5:9–11, 15) will ultimately
write a happy ending to your temporary travail.

Eliphaz is saying to Job, You're a good person. You know
it, we all know it, and presumably God knows it. That
should give you reason to look forward to a happy resolution,
because in the long run, "your piety is your confidence." In
the long run, God only gives people what they deserve. Then
he tells Job about a dream he had:

A word came to me in stealth,
My ear caught a whisper of it.
In thought-filled vision of the night,
When deep sleep falls on men . . .
A wind passed me by, making the hair of my flesh
    bristle.
It halted; his appearance was strange to me. (4:12–16)

The mysterious creature that came to him in his dream begins to speak:

> Can mortals be acquitted by God? Can Man be cleared
>   by his Maker?
> If He cannot trust His own servants, and casts
>   reproach on His angels,
> How much less those who dwell in houses of clay?
>   (4:17–19)

Eliphaz tells Job of a dream he had in which an angel tells him that even angels are not perfect. They make mistakes and God holds them accountable. How much more so will fallible human beings inevitably do something amiss, and when they do, no matter how pious and well-intentioned they are, they will be called to account.

We might think of it this way: If a popular political figure or beloved religious leader who has done a lot of good is found to have done something dishonest or unworthy, embezzling funds or betraying his marriage vows, do we ignore it? Or do we hold him even more accountable, expressing our disappointment while at the same time keeping in mind all his good deeds?

Eliphaz is saying to his friend, Job, you're a good person but you're not perfect. He adduces the familiar proverb "Man is born for mischief just as sparks fly upward" (5:7). In homage to my teacher H. L. Ginsberg, I must include his reading of that line. Ginsberg is uncomfortable translating the phrase *b'nei reshef,* children of fire, a phrase that occurs nowhere else in the Bible, as "sparks." *Reshef* is a recognizable biblical word for "fire." It occurs some half-dozen times in the Bible, notably in Song of Songs 8:6, "Love is fierce as death . . . its darts are darts of fire." But "children of fire" as a metaphor for sparks is unknown. Ginsberg emends the words to *b'nai nesher*, young eagles, and takes the verse to say "Man *gives birth* to trouble as predictably as eagles give birth to high-flying birds." Setting aside the difference between sparks and baby birds, there is a significant theological argument here, possibly a Jewish-Christian difference. Are human beings "born for mischief," that is, is it an inevitable part of our nature? Or do we "give birth to mischief"? Do we choose to do wrong? Is wrongdoing statistically highly probable, given the challenges of being human, but not innate and inevitable?

Where our translation renders the first line of the angel's remarks as "Can mortals be acquitted by God?"—that is, can a human being ever be perfect and wholly innocent?—the King James Version reads, "Can a man be more just than God?" The Hebrew text can accommodate that reading, but I don't think that is the point Eliphaz is trying to make at this juncture. Later in the book, Job's friends, gradually losing patience with him, will accuse him of insisting that he is right and God is wrong. But at this point, all Eliphaz is saying is, We all make mistakes and we are all asked to pay the price for them. Because you, Job, are a better person than most of us, you should be able to look forward to a brighter tomorrow, once you have paid your debt to God.

See how happy is the man whom God reproves,
Do not reject the discipline of the Almighty.
He injures but He binds up, He wounds but His
hands heal. (5:17–18)

Job Is Not Comforted: Chapters 6–7

At this point, I imagine Eliphaz expects Job to hug him and tell him, Thanks, I needed to hear that. I feel better now. It must have been quite a surprise to hear Job respond to his words:

A friend owes loyalty to one who fails [I prefer the
Anchor rendering: A sick man should have the
loyalty of his friends.]
Though he forsakes the fear of the Almighty.

The implication is that, even if Job somehow offended God, if his visitors were true friends, they would take his side.

My comrades are fickle, like a wadi . . .
In the heat, they disappear where they are.
(6:14–16, 17)

In the Middle East, there are only two seasons, not four. There is the rainy season, roughly October through February, and the dry season, comprising the rest of the year. The Jewish liturgical calendar reflects that, with a prayer for rain in the fall and winter and one for dew in the spring. When I spent a year studying in Israel, I noticed that the evening newscast stopped giving weather reports as of May 1; every day would be the same, sunny and hot. Job compares his friends to the streams that gush with water during the rainy season when there is water everywhere, but run dry in the summer when we need water most. You were there to celebrate with me when times were good, he says to them, but when things turned against me and I needed you, all you can do is tell me to take it like a man.

> Did I say to you, I need your gift?
> Pay a bribe for me out of your wealth? . . .
> Teach me; I will be silent. (6:22, 24)

Eliphaz had said, Think now, what innocent man ever perished? Job now challenges him: Are you telling me I'm not an innocent man, that I deserve all this misery? Verses 8–10 in chapter 6 are one of those "meaning of Hebrew uncertain" passages. If we follow the JPS translation of verse 10, "[If God would grant my wish and let me die,] then this would be my consolation as I writhe in unsparing pain, That *I did not suppress* my words against the Holy One," in preference to the most common rendering, "This would be my consolation, I would even exult in pain unsparing, for *I have not denied* the words of the Holy One," then instead of a commonplace insistence of piety on Job's part, we have what is to me one of the most moving verses in all of Scripture. Job would then be saying to his friends, If God is as great and as devoted to truth as we like to think He is, then I believe He will prefer my honesty to your flattery.

When my book *When Bad Things Happen to Good People* was published in 1981, with its suggestion that not every terrible thing that happens is God's will and that there are some parts of life that God does not control, many people were shocked and said to me something along the lines of "I thought we were supposed to accept everything as God's will and if we didn't understand some of the things He lets happen, the limitation was ours, not God's." I would answer them, "Do you find that a comforting notion, that God wanted this terrible thing [the Holocaust, the malignant tumor, the automobile accident] to happen? Does it make you feel closer to God? Does it make you feel better about God?" They would often hesitate and then say, "No, but I thought a religious person was supposed to believe it." That's when I would quote Job 6:10. Any God worth worshipping should prefer honest anger to hypocritical praise.

In chapter 7, Job stops arguing with Eliphaz and resumes his lament. Life is too short, he complains, and death is permanent.

My days fly faster than a weaver's shuttle . . .
Whoever goes down to Sheol [the netherworld where
    dead souls reside]
Does not come up,
He returns no more to his home. (7:6, 9–10)

Without reading too much into words spoken by Job out of the depths of his grief, it is worth noting that neither Job nor his visitors invoke the possibility of life after death in a better place than this world as a source of consolation. Sheol is not Heaven (or Hell). It is the repository for "used souls," since presumably our souls are not subject to physical destruction the way our bodies are. But our souls do not seem to retain anything of our memories or personality. In I Samuel 28, King Saul, anxious on the eve of a battle in which his forces are outnumbered, visits a witch–fortune teller, imploring her to summon up the ghost of Samuel from Sheol that Saul might consult him. That would imply that souls retain their personality even after death. My reading of that chapter is that there is no communication with the deceased Samuel. The witch–fortune teller fabricates the appearance and the desperate king believes her. ("What do you see?" "I see an old man in a cloak." "Yes, that's him.") Isaiah 14:11 imagines the king of Babylon after his death being greeted in Sheol by kings and tyrants who predeceased him. "You have become like us; your pomp is brought down to Sheol." But to me, Isaiah's point is the mortality of even the most powerful of men, without necessarily affirming that they retain a sense of identity after their demise. For the biblical Israelite, dead is dead.

Verses 17–18 read almost as a bitter parody of Psalm 8: "What is Man that You are mindful of him, the human being that You take note of him?" (Ps. 8:5). Job complains,

What is Man that You make much of him,

That You fix Your attention on him?

You inspect him every morning . . .

If I have sinned, what have I done to You, O watcher

of men? (7:17–18, 20)

Job calls God *notzer ha-adam*, a "man-watcher." (The phrase is Pope's in the Anchor Bible.) Where the psalmist is profoundly flattered to think that God cares about him, that his everyday deeds matter to the Almighty, Job feels persecuted by the notion. Where Job's friends are saying to him, Don't despair, God has not deserted you, He is always watching over His children, Job agrees that God is *notzer ha-adam*, watching over us, not because He loves us and cherishes what we do, but because He is eager to catch us in any small transgression and have reason to punish us. It's the difference between the ten-year-old who calls out, "Mama, come see what I can do," and the fifteen-year-old who puts a KEEP OUT sign on the door to her room and says, "Ma, would you just get off my back and leave me alone for a minute!" I think of some Orthodox Jews I know (certainly not the majority) whose religious life is dominated by the fear that God may catch them inadvertently violating one of His rules. And I remember former president Jimmy Carter confessing to having "committed adultery in [his] heart" and offended God. People like that, pious Jews and Christians alike, seem to believe in a God who is defined by His eagerness to punish us for even the smallest or most inadvertent infractions.

Job is angry at God. How shall we respond to his anger? Does it enhance or does it lessen our opinion of him? Personally, I find it heroic. I admire his honesty and integrity, his unwillingness to pretend a piety he would like to feel but cannot. (I recently read a book by a prominent Orthodox rabbi entitled *The God Who Hates Lies.*) And I am disappointed in voices in Jewish tradition that condemn him for it. One respected midrash, usually dated to the thirteenth century but containing earlier material, says, "Job, when smitten, rebelled. But Abraham, David, and Hezekiah accepted their misfortune without complaint." Another says, "Had Job not complained against God, he would have been counted among the greatest of the pious."

Is it ever acceptable to be angry at God? I would suggest that it is not only acceptable, it may be one of the hallmarks of a truly religious person. It puts honesty ahead of flattery. A few years ago, I heard a lecture by my favorite biblical scholar alive today, Professor Avivah Zornberg of Jerusalem. Professor Zornberg was raised in a traditional Jewish home in England and knows the Bible and traditional commentaries well. She also has a Ph.D. in literature from Cambridge and is well versed in Freudian psychology, and she brings all of these disciplines to bear in her biblical studies. Her talk that day was on the opening chapters of Deuteronomy, Moses's farewell speech to the Israelite people.

Zornberg pointed out that in those opening chapters, Moses does something completely out of character. He complains about God. He says that God has been unfair to him, not permitting him to enter the Land of Israel with the rest of the people. Several times in those first two chapters, Moses complains, "God was angry at me." We who have lived in the age of Freud may recognize that as projection. "God was angry at me" is a person's way of saying "I was angry at God but I'm not comfortable admitting it." Why does Moses hint at his anger at God? Zornberg asked. She suggested that he does it to give the Israelites permission to express their anger at God, which they immediately do. "It is because the Lord was angry with us that He brought us out of the land of Egypt to hand us over to the Amorites to wipe us out" (Deut. 1:27). If God really loved us, He would have let us remain in Egypt and sent the Egyptians out into this miserable desert. "God hates us" is the people's way of saying "We hate God for making us live in this desert and for imposing all those rules on us."

A few pages after the Israelites articulate their anger at God, Zornberg pointed out, we find something in the Torah we have never seen before: "You shall love the Lord your God with all your heart, with all your soul, with all your might" (Deut. 6:5), the familiar words that follow the recitation of Sh'ma Yisrael in the morning and evening service. Until now, we have been told in the Torah to revere God, to obey God, to honor God, to follow in God's ways, but not until now have we been told to love Him, because you cannot love someone wholeheartedly ("with all your heart") unless you feel free to be angry at that person when circumstances warrant. The wife who is afraid to complain to her husband when he does things that annoy her for fear that he will be upset with her and maybe leave her cannot truly love him wholeheartedly. She is censoring her emotions, withholding her true feelings. The adolescent who is afraid to share his feelings with his parents because he is afraid they will mock him, cannot love them. And we cannot love God with all our heart and with all our soul if we feel we have to censor our feelings, to pretend love and gratitude when we don't feel them. If we are angry at the way life has treated us but feel we can't speak out against the unfairness of God's world, we are being emotionally dishonest in our prayers. Those are honest feelings; why should we not be able to share them with God? Being angry at someone who matters to us— a parent, a lover, even God—need not shatter a relationship. Anger can be a part of an honest relationship. Ultimately I would like to think that we will come to realize that God is on our side, and not on the side of the misfortune. But in the meantime, echoing Job 6:10, I will insist that a God worth worshipping is a God who prefers honest anger to flattery.

5

The Argument Continues

Job's friends are stunned by his peevish response to Eliphaz's words of comfort. Not only has Job rebuffed their efforts at consolation, he has called into question one of their most cherished articles of faith, their belief in a good God who loves His children, rewarding virtue and obedience. Bildad, second of the friends, picks up the argument.

Bildad Defends God: Chapter 8

How long will you speak such things?
Your utterances are a mighty wind.
Will God pervert the right? Will the Almighty pervert justice?
If your sons sinned against Him,
He dispatched them for their transgression.
But if you seek God and supplicate the Almighty,
If you are blameless and upright, He will protect you.
  (8:1–6)

Bildad avoids suggesting that Job must have done something to deserve what happened to him. But we can understand him to be saying, Job, try to understand that this is not all about you. Your cattle were not stolen because you are a bad person. They were stolen because the Sabeans and Chaldeans are bad people. Stealing other people's cattle is what they do. Your children were not innocent victims who died to punish you. If your sons sinned, God struck them down for their misdeeds. Is that so hard for you to accept? You knew they were capable of it. Isn't that why you offered sacrifices on their behalf every time they threw a party, because you understood they might have done something improper?

Bildad then invokes the sages and scholars of previous generations:

> Ask the generations past, Study what their fathers
>   have searched out,
> For we are of yesterday and know nothing.
> Our days are as a shadow.
> Surely they will teach you and tell you. (8:8–10)

He is challenging Job: Do you think you're smarter than all the wise men of history put together? They believed in a righteous God; why can't you?

Job Concedes the Futility of Demanding That God Explain Himself: Chapters 9–10

Job is offended by Bildad's accusation that he is daring to judge the way God runs His world. He would never do that, not because he has complete faith in God's fairness but because he realizes it would be futile.

> Indeed I know that it is so,
> Man cannot win a suit against God.
> If he insisted on a trial with Him,
> He [God] would not answer one charge in a
>   thousand . . .
> He snatches away—who can stop Him?
> Who can say to Him, What are you doing? (9:2–3, 12)

Remember the three propositions that all participants are trying to reconcile:

> God is all-powerful.
> God is completely good and fair.
> Job is a good man.

The friends' solution is to affirm God's power and God's goodness, at which point they have no alternative except to question Job's innocence. He must have done something wrong; everybody does. "Man gives birth to mischief as sparks fly upward." Had they been versed in Freudian psychology, they might have said to their friend, Job: We recognize repression when we see it. Because you think of yourself as basically a good person, it is hard for you to acknowledge that part of you that has done wrong, so you repress it. The longer and more ardently you proclaim your innocence, the more certain we are that you must be hiding something from your conscious self. Give up your pretense of perfection, admit your flaws, throw yourself on the mercy of God, and He will forgive you.

Job, in contrast, affirms his own essential goodness, concedes God's power: "He moves mountains without their knowing it . . . commands the sun not to shine" (9:5, 7). But he challenges God's goodness. God is so powerful, Job complains, that no one can compel Him to play fair. At one point, Job says, "Would that there were an umpire between us, to lay his hand on us both" (9:33). (Unfortunately the JPS translation strikes out on this one, while the traditional commentaries get it right. The context demands that we read the first word as *lu*, "would that . . . ," rather than the Masoretic pointing of *lo*, "there is not." The author is too good a Hebrew poet to use a clumsy phrase like *lo yesh*.)

Job says, I wish there were some force beyond God (an umpire) to which I could appeal, someone who could make God play fair and follow the rules. But if there were, would God still be all-powerful? Would His omnipotence be compromised if some force could say to Him, You can't do that, and God had to heed it? The only theologically acceptable limitations on God's behavior are those He imposes on

Himself. Otherwise, who can say to Him, "What are You doing?" (9:12).

Think of it this way: If we, by our righteous behavior, could compel God to treat us well, to bless us with health and prosperity and guard our children from harm, would He still be the all-powerful Master of the Universe? Or would He be reduced to some supercomputer capable of doing awesome things beyond the capacity of any human being, but only if we tell it to? Would we have turned God into a cosmic vending machine: insert the proper number of good deeds—prayer, charity, forgiveness of those who hurt us—pull the plunger for the blessing you want, and if you don't get it, feel entitled to curse the machine and take your business elsewhere?

The question might occur to us at this point whether an all-powerful God *can* be good and whether an utterly good God could still be all-powerful. For God to be all-powerful would mean that there are no constraints on His behavior—not considerations of fairness, not considerations of compassion, not considerations of other people's opinions. He could take those factors into account before acting, but He would not *have* to heed them. Yet isn't it the definition of morality to say to oneself, There are things I am inclined to do but I cannot bring myself to do them without becoming someone other than the person I like to think of myself as being? If there are no such limits imposed on God's actions, can He still be "good"? Isn't arbitrariness a necessary dimension of omnipotence? What Job yearns for, what we all yearn for, is a God powerful enough to protect and redeem the innocent, but not so utterly powerful as to be beyond the constraints of fairness and compassion.

Job is offended by Bildad's accusation that he is looking to put God on trial. On the contrary, says Job, I want God to put *me* on trial. I want Him to produce evidence, convince me that I deserve all this misery.

> I say to God, Do not condemn me.
> Let me know with what You charge me. (10:2)

If this could happen to me without just cause, he pleads, that is not just a problem for me. It is a problem for everyone. It means that we live in a chaotic world where there is a disconnect between act and result. At this point, Job is on the brink of giving in to nihilism, the despairing conclusion that life is pointless.

> I am sick of life. It is all one.
> Therefore I say, He destroys the blameless and the
>   guilty . . .
> He mocks as the innocent fall.
> The earth is handed over to the wicked one . . .
> If it is not He, then who? (9:21–24)

Job's lament is this: If it makes no difference to God whether a person is good or bad, moral or selfish, if it is all one, if our behavior does not determine our fate at God's hand, why should it matter to us how we behave?

There is perhaps no more frightening line in all of Scripture than the words "the earth is handed over to the wicked one." I have read accounts of what it was like to live in Germany as the Nazis were coming to power. I have read narratives of people caught in the Sudanese civil war. One gets the feeling of helplessness, of inevitability, of being in the path of an unstoppable force. It is not only the fear that there is pure evil in the world. It is the even more frightening concern that there is no force capable of stopping it.

The sages of the Talmud, in one of their infrequent discussions of the book of Job, strenuously deny any possibility that "the wicked one" refers to God (BT Baba Batra 16a). They argue the point so emphatically that one is tempted to suspect that they think the poet *is* talking about God there, and they would rather not have that thought found in Holy Scripture. Whenever I reread Job, I am astonished that this book, and Ecclesiastes as well, were admitted to the canon. Did the sages recognize it as a work of genius and not want to deprive posterity of its insights? (The cover story for Ecclesiastes is that it was allegedly written by King Solomon in his old age.) Or, as some commentators believe, was it included because the authorities thought the arguments of the friends were cogent enough to quell the doubts of any latter-day Job who might suffer as he did and ask Job's questions?

When Job laments, in 9:24, "the earth is handed over to the wicked one. . . . If it is not He, then who?" is he considering the possibility that his problems are Satan's doing and not God's? That, after all, is the Fable's explanation. Job, of course, is not privy to God's wager with Satan in chapters 1 and 2. But if he and his friends share the theology of those opening chapters, why does no one respond to the question "If not He, then who?" by blaming Satan?

Do Jews believe in Satan? The only truthful answer to any question about what Jews believe is to say that some Jews believe it and others believe differently, while still others haven't given the question a lot of thought.

Does Judaism believe in Satan? If by Satan we mean a malevolent being, independent of God and working in opposition to God's purposes, more independent and more evil than the Satan of chapters 1 and 2 of the book of Job, then the answer is that Judaism has sometimes affirmed his existence and sometime denied it. Biblical Judaism for the most part does not know that Satan. The reference in Chronicles in connection with David's census, and perhaps Zechariah's vision, would be the exceptions, and they are both found in the latest books of the Bible. It would have been a gross anachronism, even if we assign a late date to the Poem of Job, for Job to have claimed, Even if I did some terrible things, that wasn't me. The devil made me do it.

But rabbinic and medieval Judaism did see Satan as real. For those later sages, Satan was behind every serious incident of misbehavior in Scripture. He tempts Eve into eating the forbidden fruit. He teaches Noah to plant a vineyard and gets him drunk. He tries to talk Abraham into rejecting God's demand that he sacrifice his son (after first persuading God to demand it). He inspires the people to build a golden calf at the foot of Mount Sinai. Whenever people do wrong, the sages attribute it to the machinations of Satan.

Many scholars attribute this change in how Jews understood the tendency of good people to sin to Israel's being sent into exile after the Temple was destroyed in 586 BCE. The majority of Jews ended up in one province or another of the Babylonian Empire, and after Babylonia was conquered by the Persians, they found themselves citizens of the Persian Empire. The book of Esther, for example, is set in the Persian court. It was at this time that Jews were exposed to the religion of the Persians, an early form of Zoroastrianism that was just emerging. Whereas Israel believed in one all-powerful God and their neighbors believed in a multiplicity of gods and worshipped either the god of the territory they lived in or the god whose worshippers seemed to flourish best, Zoroastrians followed a dualistic theology. They believed in two divine forces, a god of light and a god of darkness, a source of goodness and a source of malice, the two locked in eternal conflict with each other. The role of human beings, in this theology, was not simply to worship the god of light but to actively strengthen him by adding to the amount of goodness and light in the world. It is a little like the story that Native American elders would tell their children: There are two dogs inside each of us, a good dog and a mean dog, and they are always fighting. Which one will win? Whichever one we feed most.

There is something seductively appealing about this dualistic theology. It explains the existence of evil but exonerates God from responsibility for it. Bad things happen when the god of darkness is in charge. And it gives us a role in the effort to help good triumph over evil, more than merely cheerleading. But it has its limitations. For one thing, it posits a second divine being as powerful as God, a major departure from classic Hebrew monotheism. And it undermines our confidence in the ultimate triumph of good over evil. That may be why the prophet we know as Second Isaiah, in the same chapter in which he lauds the Persian emperor Cyrus as God's anointed who will lead to the restoration of the Jewish homeland, goes on to insist in the Name of God, "I am the Lord and there is none else. I form light and create darkness, I make peace and I create woe" (Isa. 45:7).

It seems plausible that Jews in the Persian Empire were attracted by some aspects of nascent Zoroastrianism but reluctant to compromise their faith in God's uniqueness. They resolved the conflict by "promoting" Satan from his biblical role as one of God's ministering angels to the role he would occupy in rabbinic and medieval Judaism, in Christianity, and in folklore ever since: that of God's adversary, preying on human weakness to defeat God's purposes. The only two biblical passages in which Satan acts contrary to God's will, the references in Zechariah and Chronicles, come in books dated to the Return to Zion under Persian auspices.

When people, ancient or contemporary, speak of Satan (or the devil), I hear them saying two things. First, evil exists. It is real, not something we would be able to accept as good if we knew all the facts. There is cruelty in the world; there is deceit. Second, and this is the key, the source of this evil is not within us but outside us. Satan is not a part of each of us; he is apart from us. There is nothing in us that would cause us to do bad things if this external source of corruption had not misled us.

Why did Eve eat the forbidden fruit? Satan tempted her. Why did Cain kill his brother Abel? Satan infected him with jealousy. Why did the Israelites build a golden calf in chapter 32 of Exodus? Satan led them astray. Satan's involvement on those occasions is not mentioned in the Bible, but the sages invoke him to explain them. People never seem to do wrong things of their own volition. They only do so when Satan misleads them.

This represents a stark departure from normative Jewish theology, both before and after the exile. The classic view of Judaism is that people are responsible for their choices. We are taught that God planted in each of us two complementary impulses, known in Hebrew as the *yetzer ha-tov* and the *yetzer ha-ra*, and typically translated as the impulse to do good and the impulse to do evil. I am bothered by that traditional translation, because it makes the evil we do something God put in us. I prefer to believe that God did not and does not create evil (despite Isaiah 45:7), though He created the *possibility* of evil by giving human beings free will. I would translate the two Hebrew terms as the capacity for altruism and the capacity for selfishness or the egotistical principle.

Selfishness can be evil (the adulterer, the fraudulent businessperson), but it need not be evil. My understanding of how the sages saw the *yetzer ha-ra* is based on a story in the Talmud. One day, in a certain village, they captured the *yetzer ha-ra* and imprisoned it. They said, From now on, our world will be Paradise. No one will ever do anything wrong. The next day, we are told, no one opened his store for business, no one bought or sold anything, no marriages were arranged, and no babies were conceived. All those activities, it turns out, contain an element of selfishness, without which the world could not function. So, reluctantly, they released the *yetzer ha-ra* from its captivity and went back to living in a world where it was a constant factor.

The world needs people like Mother Teresa to devote themselves unselfishly to caring for the afflicted and the neglected. But the world also needs men and women who will marry and raise families, who will plant crops and grow and sell food so that Mother Teresa can sustain those she cares for. The world needs people who will be so successful at what they do that they will be able to support Mother Teresa's work financially. The world needs doctors who will work to unravel the secrets of illness, with one eye on helping humanity and one eye on their place in medical history. When Dr. Henry Jekyll, in the Robert Louis Stevenson novella, finds a way to purge himself of his evil inclination, he creates a monster on the one hand and an ineffective weakling on the other. A complete human being needs both impulses, and needs the guidance of religion and the support of a moral community to nurture his altruistic impulse and rein in his ego.

When we blame Satan for the world's ills, we are saying, It wasn't me. It wasn't us. The devil made me do it. In their embarrassment, instead of taking responsibility for the misuse of their ego, people are externalizing it, projecting responsibility onto some mythical creature outside themselves. Haven't many of us had the experience, when we have given in to temptation, of saying to ourselves, I don't know why I did that. That's not me. That's not the person I am.

But if blaming Satan for our wrongdoing is an externalizing of our own capacity for doing wrong, a capacity that embarrasses us, how are we to understand the passages in the midrash where Satan seduces God into punishing an innocent person? Is there a latent capacity for evil in God Himself, and were the rabbis seeking to externalize it, to cleanse God of the embarrassment of being attracted to wrongdoing in a misuse of the divine ego, by claiming that when innocent people suffer, it is because Satan has led God astray? The sages come to the rescue of God's reputation by holding Satan responsible for manipulating God's sense of justice in a way that results in good people being hurt.

A passage in the midrash expands on Satan's role in persuading God to test Abraham as He tested Job, by demanding the death of his son. The story would have it that, after Isaac was born, Abraham and Sarah threw a festive party for their neighbors. Satan came to Abraham's tent disguised as a poor beggar, asking for a morsel of bread. But Sarah was busy nursing Isaac and Abraham was occupied seeing to his guests, and no one took heed of the beggar at the door. (The midrash warns us that "Satan is always present when no poor people are invited to a celebration.") Satan then went to God and complained, "You have blessed Abraham with so much, but he could not spare a slice of bread for a starving beggar. Such a man You call Your faithful servant?" God then resolves to prove Satan wrong and Abraham worthy of His trust by arranging the test of Abraham's loyalty.

Another midrash pictures Satan saying to God, "Isn't it sufficient that the righteous will enjoy the rewards of the World to Come? Why should they have a greater share of the good things of this world? Spread pain and pleasure more evenly in this life, and save the real rewards for the next life."

As I understand these stories, the sages, like the author of the Poem of Job, are trying to reconcile their faith in God's uncompromised goodness with the reality of good people suffering and bad people getting away with selfishness. They do it in part by seeing the misfortunes of the righteous as the misapplication of God's commitment to justice. Abraham rejected a beggar because he was busy at a party? I will teach him a lesson. Good people are too concerned with their comfort and prosperity in this world? I will remind them of what their priorities should be.

Job knows nothing of Satan. He has outgrown the idea of Satan as God's spy, as in the Fable, and understandably is unacquainted with the rabbinic-medieval notion of Satan as the Tempter, the cause outside ourselves of everything we do wrong. For him, there is only God, and it is to God that he now turns in a beautiful, deeply moving speech that forms the middle section of chapter 10. He says to God, You formed me so lovingly. You guided me through the miraculous process by which an embryo becomes a human being. Why did You do that if You knew that the end of the story would see You discard me in shame?

> Your hands shaped and formed me . . .
> You poured me out like milk, congealed me like
>   cheese.
> You clothed me with skin and flesh and wove me of
>   bones and sinews.
> You bestowed on me life and care . . .
> Yet these things You hid in Your heart . . .
> To watch me when I sinned and not clear me of my
>   iniquity. (10:8, 10–14, 16)

Zophar Takes His Turn: Chapter 11

There remains only Zophar, third and last of the visitors to speak. One commentator summarizes Zophar's remarks by writing, "There is little new to say, however many ways there are to say it." Zophar repeats the argument that God is wiser than we are, and it is not for us to question Him. One almost wonders why Zophar is even there, unless there is something in the human psyche that is more comfortable with three actors than with two or four. Think of all the children's stories where things come in threes: three bears, three pigs, three blind mice. Think of all the tales of landowners with three sons, princesses with three suitors. It may be that our minds respond to dealing with one extreme, followed by the other extreme, and then a satisfying resolution. To offer a comparison that may never have been made before in the history of literature, Goldilocks's experience with the porridge is surprisingly similar to Hegel's doctrine of thesis/antithesis/synthesis. But in the book of Job, the third statement seems more of an afterthought than a satisfying resolution.

Job Has the Last Word: Chapters 12–14

Job now concludes the first cycle of speeches with a long oration in three parts, one part addressed to the friends, a second part to God, and the third a spoken lament on the brevity of life.

> Indeed you are the voice of the people, and wisdom
>   will die with you.
> But I, like you, have a mind and am not less than you.
> Who does not know such things?
> But ask the beasts and they will teach you,
> The birds of the sky, they will tell you . . .
> That the hand of the Lord has done this.
>
>   (12:2–3, 7, 8, 9)

(I would love to read "*tamut* [wisdom] *will die* with you," not as a verb, to die, but as a noun meaning wholeness, totality, from the Hebrew *tam*, "complete," so that the phrase would read "all wisdom is with you." The phrase "wisdom will die with you" strikes me as a strange image. Unfortunately, *tamut* in that sense never appears in the Bible. Then again, the author of Job uses so many words that appear nowhere else, so perhaps . . .)

It is not clear just what Job has in mind in calling up images of birds and beasts. Following Gordis's interpretation in his commentary *The Book of God and Man*, these lines make the most sense if we hear a note of sarcasm in Job's words. He challenges his friends: Since you will never convince me that there is moral order in the world, with people getting what they deserve, you try to distract me with these descriptions of natural order, the beauty and richness of Nature, where everything has its place. Then you claim, without logic or evidence, that the same God who fashioned the perfection of Nature imposed that same perfection on the moral world.

But Job is not so easily persuaded. "Truly the ear tests arguments as the palate tests food" (12:11). Just as his mouth can recognize spoiled food, his mind can recognize shoddy reasoning, and the friends' arguments are unconvincing. For one thing, the same world of Nature that can be so impressive and orderly can turn destructive in a moment. When God holds back the waters, the streams dry up. When He lets them loose, they flood the land (12:15). And just as natural forces, let loose, can wreak havoc on a land, human rulers can lose their minds or be carried away by ambition and do great damage: "Erring and causing to err are from Him" (12:16), a point extended in the verses that follow.

Like many critics, I am suspicious of the reference to God as YHWH in verse 9: "the hand of the Lord [YHWH] has done this." It is the only use of that special name of God in the entire poem, though it is used freely in the Fable. YHWH is God's personal, intimate name used in His dealing with the Israelites. It was deemed so holy that, to this day, observant Jews do not pronounce it but use substitutes. The author of the Poem has been scrupulous in avoiding any hint that Job, Eliphaz, or the others are Jewish. They do not have Hebrew names, they live in foreign lands, they never allude to the Exodus from Egypt in discussing God's beneficence. There are no references to God's promises to the patriarchs or to the Covenant at Sinai, with its warnings along with its promises. With one crucial exception, to which we will come at the climax of the book, there is nothing to connect the theological discourse to anything in the Torah. Job's problems are the problems of Everyman, not only of Jews. It would be passing strange for the author to violate that rule in this casual context. Most likely, a scribe, unaware of the point the author was making, unconsciously substituted the personal name of God for the more universal names indicating divinity, like El, Elohim, and Shaddai.

But if Job the person is not Jewish, Job the book is a thoroughly Jewish book, beginning with its arrogating to itself the right to challenge and question God on moral grounds. Israel, as its name ("the God-wrestler") implies, has always been a people who not only sought to serve God but has struggled with God, and not only because of the bad things that happened to it.

Ancient Israel had no monopoly on suffering, but Israel's response to misfortune was different from that of its neighbors. The Babylonian steamroller that demolished the Temple of Jerusalem also crushed all the other little kingdoms of that part of the world. Israel was unique not in its fate but in its response. Edomites and Moabites who saw the power of Babylon acknowledged that the god of the Babylonians must be stronger than the gods they were accustomed to worshipping, gods who were not able to protect them, and they shifted their allegiance. Superior power compelled obedience. Only the Israelites, contemplating the destruction of their homeland and sacred Temple, refused to do that, saying to themselves (as Jeremiah had warned them), God did this to us because we violated His covenant. We were unfaithful and this is our punishment. (It was a response that made Israel's survival as a separate people possible in the sixth century BCE. It would serve less well—indeed, it would strike most of us as grotesque—when used to explain the Holocaust.) Other nations worshipped a powerful god, the most powerful they could find. Israel served a God who was both powerful and just, and they would spend the next 2,500 years trying to reconcile those two attributes with each other and with the collective suffering of the Jewish people and the anguish of so many individual Jews.

Is there a uniquely Jewish sensibility when it comes to talking about God? Job is not Jewish, but the author who put words in his mouth was. Let me suggest that at the core of Jewish God-talk is the unshakable conviction that God's most dominant attribute is His commitment to justice rather than power. Earthly kings lust for power, for total control, and are prepared to sacrifice justice, to hurt innocent people, to hold on to power. But as far as the God of Israel is concerned, in a conflict between justice and power, justice will prevail. God will not do wrong. That more than anything gives Job reason to hope.

A thoroughly unfair cliché would have it that Judaism is a religion of law whereas Christianity is a religion of love. But we find rules and we find condemnations of rule-breakers in Christianity (religion has to have standards), and we find a frequent emphasis on the need for divine and human forgiveness in Judaism. What is Yom Kippur about if not an articulation of our turning to God to accept us despite our all-too-human failings? The rabbis taught us long ago that a world of strict justice, with no allowances for human weakness, would be an unlivable world. An exercise of the rabbinic imagination adds yet another dimension to that. One of the sages asks, "Does God pray?" His answer: God does indeed pray, and His prayer is "May it be My will that My attribute of compassion overrule My attribute of justice." Justice is more of a primary divine attribute than power, but divine compassion is on a par with divine justice.

Job has been compared to Shakespeare's King Lear. Both men are powerful figures stripped of their wealth and power. Both are bereaved, both are afflicted, and both cry out their rage against an unfair world. But where Lear includes God among those forces that torment him ("As flies to wanton boys are we to the gods; they kill us for their sport"; the original King Lear was probably a pagan, but that need not have colored Shakespeare's character), Job never gives up hope that God's sense of justice will prevail over the arbitrary exercise of divine power.

Despite what I wrote earlier to the effect that more advanced spiritual development need not mean a later date of composition, it is tempting to see the universality of Job, expressed through Jewish eyes, as pointing to a post-exilic origin. There is no Israelite parochialism here, no asumption that everyone we are concerned with is Jewish. Job's cry is not "Why do these things happen to us, God's people?" but "Why do these things happen at all?" It is a perspective that might well have arisen in a Jewish community living in exile among other exiles, or in a restored Zion shared with other ethnic groups imported by Babylonia after 586 BCE, refugees and war victims just as the Israelites were.

Job continues:

> Indeed I would speak to the Almighty, I insist on
>   arguing with God.
> But you invent lies, all of you are quacks.
> If you would only keep quiet, it would be considered
>   wisdom on your part . . .
> Will you speak deceitfully for Him? Will you plead
>   God's cause? . . .
> He will surely reprove you if in your hearts you are
>   partial toward Him . . .
> I will take my life in my hands,
> He may slay me, I may have no hope,
> Yet I will argue my case before Him.
> In this too is my salvation: that no impious man can
>   come into His presence. (13:3–5, 7–8, 10, 14–15)

Verse 15 is familiar to many churchgoers and readers of the King James translation: "Though He slay me, yet will I trust in Him." It is a beautiful line and a beautiful thought. It can be taken as saying to God, "I love You at least as much as You love me. No matter what You do to me, I will always love You." Those words can be an expression of the deepest, truest love, or they can be the outlook of a dependent person without the self-respect to stand up for his or her rights. But it is hard to believe that that is what Job is saying. Job believes in God but is in no mood to do God any favors. He would have no problem loving God if God would only play fair. In the face of rampant unfairness, that love and faith are hard to come by. When Job says in 13:16, "In this is my salvation, that no impious person can come into His presence," I hear echoes of 6:10: If God is a God worth worshipping, He will prefer honest anger to calculated flattery. On those grounds, I prefer the JPS reading, "I may have no hope." (Notice the "may," which is not explicit in the Hebrew.)

Job then ceases arguing with his visitors and turns directly to God, as if to emphasize that his quarrel is not with well-meaning friends over their theology, but with God Himself over the way He runs His world.

> Remove Your hand from me, let not Your terror
> frighten me.
> Then summon me and I will respond,
> Or I will speak and You reply to me:
> How many are my iniquities and sins?
> Advise me of my transgressions.
> Why do You hide Your face and treat me like an
> enemy?
> Will You harass a driven leaf . . .
> That You decree for me bitter things and make me
> answer for the iniquities of my youth? (13:21–26)

In other words, Job is saying to God: If I am important enough for You to keep track of my every mistake and punish me for them, then am I not worth five minutes of Your time to tell me what I am being punished for? And if I am too insignificant to merit Your personal attention, then why am I important enough for You to measure out my punishment?

Chapter 14 is among the most beautiful sections of the entire book. It reads equally well in Hebrew or in English. Job laments the brevity of life and challenges God: If life is so short, why do You have to spoil it by calling down punishment on us for every trivial violation? You are eternal, but You will be rid of us soon enough.

> Man born of woman is short-lived and sated with
> trouble,
> He blossoms like a flower and withers.
> He vanishes like a shadow and does not endure.
> Do You fix Your gaze on such a one and bring me to
> trial against You?
> [JPS reads, "Will you go to law with me?"]
> Turn away from him, that he may be at ease
> Until like a hireling, he finishes out his day.
>   (14:1–3, 6)

Although no one has raised the prospect of life after death as compensation for unjust suffering or of a person's resurrection to a second go at life—it seems the notion probably did not exist in Israel before the time of the Maccabees and the book of Daniel—Job anticipates it and rejects it.

> There is hope for a tree:
> If it is cut down, it will renew itself. Its shoots will
> not cease.

> If its roots are old in the earth and its stump dies in
>   the ground,
> At the scent of water, it will bud and produce
>   branches like a sapling.
> But mortals languish and die, Man expires, where
>   is he? . . .
> His sons attain honor and he does not know it.
>   (14:7–10, 21)

With Job, I feel the special poignancy of that last line. The most painful aspect of mortality is that a person will not live to see his or her children grow old. (Clearly this is not Job of the Fable with whom we are dealing. He had no surviving children. This is Job as Everyman.)

So ends the first cycle of speeches. The friends have invoked tradition and the widely held consensus that God is great, that God knows us better than we know ourselves, and that He punishes only when He has a reason to punish. If Job would just stop insisting on his innocence—what human being is perfect?—and throw himself on the mercy of God, then a merciful God will likely forgive him. Don't let one week of misery outweigh the satisfaction of years of piety.

In contrast to the friends' theoretical arguments, Job offers his own experience. You cite abstract beliefs, he tells them, theological generalities, undocumented opinions based on nothing more than the fact that most people agree with you. I offer the real, hard, undeniable facts of my bereavement and my illness, and to me, these are more persuasive than your theories. (The friends' position calls to mind Chico Marx's line in the movie *Duck Soup:* "Who are you going to believe, me or your own eyes?")

While the remarks have occasionally been pointed, for the most part they have been respectful. The friends genuinely want to comfort Job, not to convert him, and more than anything else, Job wants a hearing. He would rather be told what he has done wrong than to have God concede that He is wrong and Job is right.

Much of that will change in the second cycle.

6

The Argument Gets Personal

Chapters 15–21

To this point, Job's friends have been saying to him, You are basically a good person. Not perfect perhaps, but definitely good. Because of that, and because God is just, there is every reason to believe that things will work out well for you in the end. We recognize this as a slightly more sophisticated version of the theology of the Fable, minus Satan and the wager: Hold on to your faith, trust in God, and there will be a happy ending. Righteousness doesn't win every round. Mischief and misfortune do their damage. But if we are patient, we will ultimately see justice prevail. When Job was not comforted by these words, the friends seemed at first to ask themselves, What is wrong with the way we are presenting our arguments that Job is unmoved by them? But a note of frustration increasingly creeps into their remarks, and now their message becomes, What is wrong with Job that he can't see the merit of what we are saying? Newsom characterizes their position as evolving from confidence in

Job's innocence and ultimate vindication (as in chapter 5) to wondering if there might be some unacknowledged sin on Job's part (as in chapter 11) to asserting that his stubbornness and arrogance are themselves proof of his impiety (in chapter 15).

Job, You're Too Young to Teach Us About the World: Chapter 15

In his second set of remarks, Eliphaz criticizes Job in much stronger terms than we have heard previously:

> Does a wise man answer with windy opinions?
> Should he argue with useless talk, with words of no
> worth?
> Have you listened in on the council of God?
> Have you sole possession of wisdom?
> What do you know that we do not know?
> Among us are gray-haired men, older than your father.
> (15:1, 2, 6–10)

No longer making allowances for the fact that Job is speaking out of pain and bereavement, he accuses Job of arrogance born of immaturity. He hasn't lived long enough to be an expert on the fairness of God's world and claim to be wiser than his elders, a gross violation of the ethics of that age.

Eliphaz, who had previously cited a dream he had (4:12–21) in which an angel told him that even angels are not immune to doing wrong and offending God, refers back to that message in almost the same words. Then he makes a new point, warning Job that the man who rebels against God (and presumably against the traditional understanding of God) calls down a punishment on himself as bad as anything God might do to him. What would that punishment be? He condemns himself to a life of waiting for God's lightning bolt to find him, never knowing when it might strike. He goes to bed at night never knowing if this will be his last night on earth. He wakes up in the morning wondering if this will be the day God gets around to punishing him. Eliphaz warns Job, as a friend, to give up this unseemly self-righteousness.

> The wicked man writhes in torment all his days . . .
> He is never sure he will come back from the dark . . .
> Troubles terrify him, anxiety overpowers him
> Like a king expecting a siege,
> For he has raised his arm against God.
>
> (15:20, 22, 24–25)

Job Ignores Eliphaz and Turns Directly to God: Chapters 16–17

Beginning with Job's reply in chapter 16, the Hebrew text becomes harder to understand, at times putting words in one speaker's mouth that contradict what he has been saying and would fit better as someone else's remarks, and not infrequently verging on the unintelligible. The majority of critics blame careless copyists who transcribed poetry they did not understand or pious scribes who tried to mitigate what struck them as heresy. My own inclination is to give the text the benefit of the doubt wherever possible. (I am reminded of the midterm exam in my freshman humanities class in college. It consisted of two questions: [1] Of all the books we have read this semester, which one did you enjoy least? [2] To what limitation in yourself do you attribute this inability to appreciate an acknowledged classic?) What follows is my best effort to make sense of a difficult text, aided by the insights of some of the finest biblical scholars. Sometimes, when a speaker's remarks seem inconsistent with what he has been saying previously (for example, Job's words in 17:9, "The righteous man holds to his way; he whose hands are clean grows stronger"—that doesn't sound like Job), we can take them as a mocking paraphrase of what the friends have been saying, which he will then set out to refute, rather than dismiss them as verses out of place or a pious addition. Gordis, for example, in his commentary on the baffling book of Ecclesiastes, uses this technique to great effect to make sense of confusing passages.

Job begins his response to Eliphaz by saying,

I would also talk like you if you were in my place . . .
I would encourage you with words. (16:4–5)

But beyond those words of dismissal, he does not address himself to Eliphaz's comments. His quarrel is with God, not with three pious neighbors. He goes on to lament his fate and articulate his suffering, and then late in the chapter he says,

> Surely now my witness is in heaven
> He who can testify for me is on high . . .
> Let Him arbitrate between man and God as between
> one man and another. (16: 9, 21)

What does Job have in mind when he speaks of a witness in Heaven? Is he again wishing that there were some entity more powerful than God (a cosmic law of justice, perhaps, which even God would have to respect), as in 9:33 when he wished that there were an umpire between him and God? Or is he saying that if God had to testify under oath, He would support Job's claims? I take his words to mean, Not only is God the judge in my case, not only is He the defendant whom I accuse of doing harm without cause. He is also the chief witness for the defense. If summoned, He would testify to my righteousness.

Two verses in Job's lament deserve close attention. The first, 16:18, reads "Earth, do not cover my blood." It has been used as the title of at least one Holocaust memoir and appears as the superscription in any number of local Holocaust memorials. I find in it an echo of God's words to Cain in Genesis 4:10, "your brother's blood cries out to Me from the ground," and of the law in Deuteronomy 21:1–9. If a corpse is found and the murderer cannot be identified, a complicated ritual of expiation must be performed, at the end of which the town elders proclaim, "Absolve, O Lord, Your people Israel and let not the blood of the innocent remain among Your people." The unrequited blood of an innocent victim is an affront to God, the Author of Life, and it is a violation of human dignity to try to cover up the offense by burying it out of sight. When Job cries out, "Earth, do not cover my blood," he may be challenging God to live up to His own declared standards and not ignore the death of innocent people.

And in 17:6, Job says,

> He made me a byword among people,
> I have become like Tophet of old.

Pope, in his Anchor commentary, misreads the significance of the obscure word "Tophet" and, relying on an Aramaic cognate, translates those last words as "one in whose face people spit." I would connect Tophet to a verse in Jeremiah 7:31, condemning the Israelites for turning to pagan practices. The prophet says, in God's name, "they have built the shrine of Tophet in the valley of Ben-Hinnom to burn their sons and daughters in fire." We know from archaeological findings that the valley of Ben-Hinnom, adjacent to the Temple Mount in Jerusalem (the name would pass into the language as Gehenna and would come to symbolize the fires of Hell), was used for the burning of corpses, presumably bearers of infection who would not be fit to be buried in a family crypt, and also for the dreadful rite of offering one's firstborn child to the gods of darkness, in a superstitious effort to buy their favor. It was viewed with abhorrence by decent Israelites. Job may be saying that God, by killing his children, by making his home a place where children died, has turned him into someone as repulsive, as horrifying, as the Tophet in the valley of Hinnom. Critics who disagree note the unlikelihood of the author referring to a specifically Israelite site. The reference would have been instantly recognizable to Israelite readers but inappropriate in the mouth of a resident of Uz. If my reading is correct, we once again encounter the ambiguity of an Israelite reference, a Jewish perspective, on the part of a gentile protagonist. I can imagine the Israelite author of Job experiencing a sense of horror bordering on blasphemy at an image that would portray the God of Israel as no better than the bloodthirsty pagan gods who demanded human sacrifices. For Job to accuse God of turning his home into another Tophet is a serious charge.

Bildad Rebukes Job for Asking an Unsettling Question: Chapter 18

It is now Bildad's turn to defend the conventional theology of their time. Where Eliphaz excoriated Job for presuming to be wiser than the best minds of generations past, Bildad accuses him of considering his personal fate more important than what happens to all the other people on the planet. Bildad insists that, in the long run, punishment catches up with the wicked, a point he makes at great length and with considerable eloquence.

> Indeed the light of the wicked fails . . .
> His schemes overthrow him, he is led by his feet into
>   a trap . . .
> Terror assaults him on all sides.
> He is thrust from light into darkness, driven from the
>   world. (18:5, 7–8, 11, 18)

Unfortunately it ignores Job's complaint that the well-deserved misery of the wicked doesn't balance the undeserved suffering of the innocent at God's hand.

Bildad seems to be making an argument we have not heard before. When he challenges Job, "Will earth's order be disrupted for your sake?" (18:4), he is saying, in effect, How dare you disturb us with your reality? Don't you understand that relying on God to protect the innocent and punish the wicked is what helps us go on with our daily lives? That is what lets us close our eyes and go to sleep at night. That is what gives us the courage to wake up in the morning and face the world. That is why we feel safe bringing children into this world and letting ourselves love them. We do it because we trust God to keep them and us safe. And you have the nerve to say to us that maybe God is not like that? Like Dostoevsky's Grand Inquisitor in *The Brothers Karamazov*, who tells Jesus that people don't want freedom, they want miracle, mysticism, and authority, Bildad is saying to Job, We and everyone like us are not interested in truth when it comes to God. We don't go to church and synagogue for a theology seminar. We go to be reassured that God is a loving Father who will protect us, and when He chastises us, it is for our own good and because we deserve it. If you try to tell us, based on your own atypical experience, that such a God does not exist, we will not listen to you.

The 1985 made-for-TV movie *Shadowlands* tells of events late in the life of C. S. Lewis. Lewis had been a renowned scholar of English literature at Oxford and was perhaps the most eloquent spokesman for Christian faith in Great Britain. He was also a lifelong bachelor. As the movie begins, we see Lewis speaking to an audience on the question of why God lets good people suffer. To him, it is God's way of helping us become deeper, wiser, stronger people. Pain, we hear him tell his listeners, is the chisel the divine Sculptor uses to shape us into the people He envisions us as capable of being.

Shortly after that, Lewis meets and unexpectedly falls in love with an American woman, Joy Davidman, and they marry, inspiring his book *Surprised by Joy*. They are happy together for several years, until Joy falls ill with bone cancer. Watching the woman he loves die an agonizing, painful death, Lewis can no longer believe and teach that "pain is the chisel God uses to perfect us." He acknowledges that the suffering of the righteous is a mystery beyond our understanding. It must have been hard for him to disavow a position he had held so publicly for so long, but seeing the woman he loves in agony, he has to concede "this cannot be

God's will." The reality of his life has overpowered his theology, and to his credit, he has the integrity to give up what he believed and taught for years. (I can appreciate how hard that was, having gone through the same process under similar circumstances.) In choosing the truth of real life over the comfortable illusion of traditional belief, he does something Job's friends are incapable of doing.

Bildad, in his remarks to Job, may even be implying: In olden times, people sacrificed their children to God to keep God on their side. Soldiers have sacrificed their lives in battle for the safety and security of their country. People sacrifice so many things precious to them as a token of their love of God. They give up dreams of fame and fortune to devote their lives to caring for the needy. They spurn offers of great wealth rather than compromise their ethical values. Priests and nuns take on vows of celibacy, sacrificing the prospect of sexual fulfillment as their love gift to God. Can't you give up your tiresome protestations of innocence and offer yourself and your children as a sacrifice so that the rest of the world can see you maintaining your faith and go on believing in a God who keeps good people safe? And Job can be seen as responding, No, I will not lie to God and I will not lie about God. I will not base my life and faith on what I now know to be a lie.

Toward the end of his remarks, Bildad gets so carried away by thoughts of the punishments awaiting evildoers (why are so many more people bothered when bad people get away with murder than when good people suffer unjustly?

I've lost count of the people who have urged me to write a book entitled *When Good Things Happen to Bad People*) that he conjures up the worst punishment he can imagine for them:

> He has no seed or breed among his people,
> No survivor where once he lived. (18:19)

It would indeed be the ultimate punishment in the ancient world to have no children to carry on one's name and line. It would give death yet another dimension of finality, removing a person not only from today's world but from tomorrow's as well. Biblical Israel had elaborate provisions to try to avoid that. But Bildad seems blind to the impact those words would have on the recently bereaved Job. Are his friends really so angry at Job that they would utter words calculated to wound him where he is most vulnerable? Or have they left Job's case behind and are now dealing with divine reward and punishment in general? Why on earth would they think that it might comfort Job to be lectured about the ultimate downfall of the wicked (unless the friends are trying to warn him that if he continues on his heretical path, that will be his fate)?

Job's Plea for a Redeemer: Chapter 19

Job responds to Bildad in chapter 19 in an outburst that is more despairing than anything we have yet heard from him. This is no longer Job from the land of Uz crying out.

This is Everyman who has had a pleasant life snatched from him and replaced with misery and loss. The real-life Job has no surviving children and no servants, but nonetheless in chapter 19 he laments,

> My friends have forgotten me,
> My dependents and maidservants respond to me as a
>   stranger.
> Summon my servant but he does not respond . . .
> My odor is repulsive to my wife, I am loathsome to
>   my children. (19:15–17)

He complains that God has afflicted him in every way possible, and then he reproaches his friends for siding with that cruel, unjust, powerful God rather than with their innocent, afflicted friend:

> Know that God has wronged me . . .
> Pity me! Pity me! You are my friends,
> For the hand of God has struck me.
> Why do you punish me as God does? (19:6, 21–22)

Job goes on:

> O that my words were written down,
> Incised on a stone forever
> With an iron stylus and lead . . . (19:23–24)

And then we come to one of the most challenging verses in the entire book. The Hebrew of 19:25 can be translated in words familiar to most of us:

> For I know that my Redeemer lives;
> In the end, he will testify on earth.

Or it can mean:

> Then I might find redemption in my lifetime,
> Vindicated while I am still here on earth.

Predictably, the more traditionally inclined commentators are drawn to the former, more God-affirming interpretation, while those whose souls resonate more to Job's skepticism (like me, for one) prefer the "prove it to me" approach of the latter. Gordis, among the traditionalists, writes, "From the depths of despair, Job soars to the heights of faith . . . as Job appeals from God to God." Gordis sees a steady progression from chapter 9, when Job asks for an umpire to intercede between him and God and make God play by the rules, to chapter 16, where Job invokes God as an impartial witness to declare that there is no case to be made against him, to his seeing God here, in chapter 19, as his *go'el*, his Redeemer, who is so fundamentally committed to justice and fairness that in the end He will feel obliged to take Job's side to set things right.

Who or what is this Redeemer whom Job either believes in or longs to see? What is the role of a *go'el* in the Bible? A *go'el* is a fixer, a person who sees something that is wrong, something that is unfair, and feels obliged to do something about it. In today's world, a *go'el* can be someone who offers to pay off the mortgage for a neighbor or relative so that she won't lose her home, or someone who intervenes to stop a bully. In the biblical context, the concept of *go'el* as redeemer has three shades of meaning, all of them connected to the notion of taking an unacceptable situation and setting it right and none of them carrying the freight of the understanding of that term that would emerge in later Christianity, the notion of a Redeemer who saves sinful souls from the punishment of hellfire.

First, a *go'el* can be an avenger. In pre-monarchic Israel, at a time when there was no central judicial authority and every community had to impose justice in its own way, the custom prevailed, and is recognized in the Torah, that if someone murdered another person, a relative of the deceased was entitled, indeed obliged, to avenge the death by killing the murderer. He was known as the *go'el ha-dam*, the "blood avenger." It was considered a gross impropriety, an offense against God and against the dignity of the victim, to leave innocent blood unrequited (see Deut. 19:11–12). Biblical law further decreed that the killing stop there. The murderer's relatives had no right to avenge themselves on the *go'el*, whose act was considered morally and legally justified. It would be a significant step forward when later generations gave to the state that responsibility for putting murderers to death and took the element of personal vengeance out of it.

A second task of a *go'el*, unattested to in the Torah but alluded to in the prophetic and wisdom literature, was to ransom family members who had been taken captive in war or had sunk so badly into debt that they had to sell themselves as slaves (not *Uncle Tom's Cabin*–style slaves, where one human being owns another, but indentured servants for a fixed period of time to work off a debt). A family member who had the means could redeem his relative from servitude by paying his bills. Thus Jeremiah promises an exiled Judea, "He who scattered Israel will gather them. . . . The Lord will redeem [*g'alo*, from the same root as *go'el*] him from one too strong for him" (Jer. 31:10–11).

A final function of the *go'el* is spelled out in Leviticus 25:25–30. The Torah, in that chapter, goes to great lengths to ensure that there never arises in Israel a class of permanently poor, landless individuals, driven by bad luck or bad harvests to sell their homes and fields, leaving them with no way to earn a living. "If your kinsman is in straits and has to sell his home and field, his relative shall act as a *go'el* and redeem what his kinsman has sold."

A *go'el*, then, is someone who intervenes when an unjust or intolerable situation has come about and takes on himself the responsibility for setting things right. He is obliged to do this for a kinsman even if the kinsman's situation is the result of his own action. It is to this dimension of God, a God who cannot tolerate the reduction of a human being, fashioned in His image, to less than human status, that Job may be appealing. Job, in his extremity, is calling on God, saying, "I have no one left. I am without family. My friends have deserted me. You who are the Father of all humanity, is it not Your obligation to atone for my children's deaths as their *go'el* and to extract me from my current situation as my *go'el*?"

Zophar Warns Us Not to Envy the Wicked: Chapter 20

I t is left to poor Zophar, in chapter 20, to take his turn in a vain effort to say something to Job that has not already been said and repeated. His message:

> Do you not know this, that from time immemorial,
> Since man was first set on earth,
> The joy of the wicked has been brief? . . .
> Though evil is sweet to his taste,
> His food in his bowels turns to venom within him.
>
> (20:4–5, 12–14)

In other words, do not envy the wicked. They will not enjoy their ill-gotten gains for long. No matter how much they accumulate, their conscience will trouble them and their wealth will not last. I can picture Job, Eliphaz, and Bildad looking at Zophar and saying to themselves, Why is he saying that? I don't recall anyone saying that we *should* envy the wicked. But now Job, perhaps exasperated by his friends' lack of sympathy for what he has gone through and by the superficiality of their theological affirmations, proceeds to do exactly that, to make a case in favor of the wicked. It may be that Job has been pushed over the edge. Anticipating consolation, he has heard pious platitudes. Hoping for sympathy, he has heard only warnings of what will happen to him if he persists in his complaints. In desperation as the second cycle of speeches draws to a close, Job breaks down and says, Right now, I *do* envy the wicked. I would rather be an evil person, living at ease with my family around me, than have to suffer bereavement so that people will praise me at my funeral.

Job's Last Words in the Second Cycle

Why should I not lose my patience?
Look at me and be appalled.
Why do the wicked live on, prosper and grow wealthy?
Their children are with them always
And they see their children's children.
Their homes are secure, without fear . . .
They spend their days in happiness and go down to
     Sheol in peace.
They say to God, "Leave us alone,
We do not want to learn your ways."

　(21:4–5, 7–9, 13–14)

And on that note, the second cycle of speeches is concluded. In it, we have seen the friends grow colder, more critical, and less sympathetic. And we have seen Job driven to the edge of despair. Things will soon change.

7

A Confusion, a Perplexity, and a Surprising Climax

Chapters 22–31

To this point, the ideas put forth by Job and his visitors, and the theological assumptions behind them, have often been a challenge to understand, but at least the structure of the book has been clear. Job pours out his heart and his friends take turns either comforting or enlightening him. We always know who is speaking and which side he is on. Over the next several chapters, even that clarity disappears. Words are attributed to speakers that contradict the positions they have held until now. Chapters 22 and 23 are cut from the same cloth as the exchanges that preceded them, though the tone of Eliphaz's remarks in chapter 22 is conspicuously less friendly. But these will be the last chapters where we can be confident that we know who is speaking and what point he is trying to make.

Many readers will be perplexed by the gratuitously nasty

tone of Eliphaz's remarks in his third discourse, found in chapter 22:

> You know that your wickedness is great
> And that your iniquities have no limits.
> You exact pledges from your fellow man without
>   reason
> And leave them naked, stripped of their clothes.
> [That is, when you lend someone money, you take his
>   clothing to ensure repayment.]
> You do not give the thirsty water to drink,
> You deny bread to the hungry . . .
> You have sent widows away empty-handed . . .
>   (22:5–7, 9)

Where did this come from? Until now, the argument of the friends has been: Job, we all know that you are basically a good man, and because we believe God is just, we have to believe that things will work out in the long run. At worst, they have said, Job, you're a good man, but you're only human. We all make mistakes. You must have done your share along the way and God is calling you to account. Suddenly we find Eliphaz saying, Job, you are the worst person who ever lived, exploiting the poor and the needy. No wonder God sees fit to punish you.

What is going on? What has prompted this change of attitude? Have the friends concluded that, because Job is suffering so extravagantly, he must have done something terrible to deserve it? (Since sin leads to punishment, punishment must be the result of sin.) Or is Eliphaz speaking out of frustration because Job refuses to accept his earlier arguments on God's behalf? One critic suggests that Job's challenging the accepted moral order of the universe is "the moral equivalent" of being cruel to the needy and doing all the terrible things Eliphaz accuses him of. That strikes me as forced. When I studied Job with H. L. Ginsberg many years ago, he clarified chapter 22 brilliantly in just a few sentences. He imagined Eliphaz introducing these charges by saying to Job, All day long, you have been asking God to tell you what you have done to deserve this fate. If only He would tell you what you are being punished for, you would be able to accept it. Are you serious? God has a world to run. He has millions of people to keep track of. He doesn't have time to sit down with every one of us who isn't happy with his life and give him an itemized list of his infractions:

On January 11, you ignored a needy beggar.
On February 3, you lied to your wife about where you
    had been.
On March 21, you kicked a neighbor's dog.
On June 4, you told a collector for a local charity that
    you couldn't afford to help him.

How could God ever get anything done if every day He had to explain why He was doing something to everyone who was unhappy with it? Either you believe that God keeps an accurate set of books or you don't.

The Argument Seems to Be Taking Its Toll on a Weary Job: Chapters 23–24

J ob is either unimpressed by Eliphaz's words or too weary to take them seriously, though he may be responding to them point by point in chapter 31.

> Today again my complaint is bitter,
> My strength is spent on account of my groaning.
> (23:2)

Does the phrase "today again" imply that the argument has gone on for more than one day? I'm inclined to think it is simply rhetoric.

Unmoved by Eliphaz's sarcasm—do you really expect God to present you with a list of your sins?—Job repeats that that is, in fact, precisely what he wants. How can he repent sincerely, how can he change his ways, how can he maintain his faith in God's justice, unless he knows what he has done to deserve what happened to him?

> Would that I knew how to reach Him,
> How to get to His dwelling place.
> I would set my case before Him,
> I would learn what answers He has for me.
> But if I go East, He is not there,
> West, I still do not perceive Him . . .

Would He assay me, I should emerge as pure gold,
I have not deviated from what His lips commanded.
(23:2–5, 8, 10–11)

Chapter 24 presents itself as a continuation of Job's remarks in chapter 23, but while the thoughts may fit that attribution, the language and diction seem different from anything Job has been saying to this point. The first half of the chapter is a condemnation of the wickedness of bad people and God's seeming indifference to it.

People remove boundary stones, they carry off flocks
   and pasture them . . .
They chase the needy off the roads . . .
Men groan in the city, the souls of the dying cry out,
Yet God does not respond to their prayer. (24:2, 4, 12;
   the last line is my translation, reading the final
   word as *tefillah*, prayer, rather than *tiflah*, reproach,
   as in JPS.)

Regarding the last half of the chapter, the editors of the JPS translation concede in a footnote, "From here to the end of the chapter, the translation is highly conjectural." It suggests that God does not judge human misbehavior, and describes the wicked pursuing their villainy while the righteous suffer the consequences. Verse 9 is almost certainly out of place, but the passage is redeemed by one wonderful phrase describing the wicked as *mordei or*, "rebels against the light" (24:13).

Bildad's reply in chapter 25 contains only five verses, while Zophar doesn't speak at all. Job's final statement goes on for six long chapters, during which he says things that contradict what he has said previously. It seems clear that passages are out of sequence and the coherence of the book has fallen victim to confused or careless editing. (It may be unfair to expect scribes who were not trained theologians to keep track of who said what.) Gordis, who generally strives to justify the text as we have it, here has to concede, "It is at this point that the structure of the third cycle breaks down. . . . Much of chapters 26–31 is inappropriate to Job [and] chapter 26 is irrelevant to Job's position." Pope, in the Anchor commentary, says more succinctly, "Chapters 24–27 are thoroughly scrambled."

Some scholars would attach 22:12–20 to Bildad's abbreviated remarks in chapter 25. More commonly and more persuasively, others see 26:5–14 as more likely to have been uttered by Bildad than by Job, though these verses are attributed to Job. If you are not tempted to cut and paste, you can rest in the knowledge that this section of the book is fairly inscrutable. Newsom suggests that the incoherent language of chapters 24–27 reflects the brokenness of Job's soul. "One of the frequent consequences of traumatic experience is an initial loss of language," exemplified by Job's seven days of silence in chapter 2, followed by "a more permanent estrangement from language."

I would extend her point. By this time, it is not only Job whose mind is exhausted by the effort to make sense of the inexplicable. His friends, too, seem to feel compelled to make arguments they may not fully believe in, rather than concede that Job may be right in his critique of God's justice. Their internal confusion is reflected in the incoherence of their remarks.

Along those lines, the book of Leviticus tells of the sudden death of the two oldest sons of the high priest Aaron, in response to which "Aaron was silent" (Lev. 10:1–3). Readers have to bring their own understanding of Aaron's silence. Was it humble acceptance of God's will? Was he too stunned to react? Or, as I like to believe, were the words Aaron was inclined to speak angry, even heretical words, and he kept himself from uttering them in the immediacy of the tragedy? For Newsom, that would be another example of how trauma impedes speech. Yes, "the author gives Job some of the most brilliant poetry in the book. But the brilliance of his speech is the brilliance of light reflected through shattered glass of many colors." Her comment calls to mind the suggestion of psychologist Theodor Adorno that "after Auschwitz, there can be no poetry."

The most intriguing explanation I know of is offered by Professor Joseph Koterski of Fordham University, in a series of lectures on the Wisdom Literature of the Hebrew Bible prepared for home study by the Teaching Company. Father Koterski suggests that the incoherence of chapters 24–27, where it is never clear who is saying what, reflects the breakdown of the dialogue as it comes to its end, with everyone speaking at once, interrupting one another and shouting over one another's remarks. As he sees it, the argument has run its course. Everyone has said what he has to say, and no one is any longer listening to anyone else. The book is about to move into a different mode.

Chapter 27 begins smoothly enough with an eloquent, impressive outburst on Job's part. It can be read as a continuation of 26:1–4, where Job says to his friends:

> What help have you been to those without strength?
> What advice have you given the unwise? (26:2–3)

We can then proceed to 27:2, where Job continues. I love this passage, for its language as much as for its theology. No matter how often I read it, I am thrilled by the clarity and passion of Job's words. One senses that the book is moving toward its climax.

> By God who deprived me of justice,
> By Shaddai who has embittered my life,
> As long as there is life in me,
> And God's breath is in my nostrils,
> My lips will speak no wrong
> Nor my tongue utter deceit.
> Far be it from me to say that You are right.
> Until I die, I will maintain my integrity. (27:2–5)

This is Job at his best, challenging the God he continues to believe in to live up to His own professed standards of truth and justice. But these are the last words in chapter 27 that sound like Job. The remaining seventeen verses sound more like one of his three friends. (Perhaps it is Zophar's missing speech, as Pope proposes.)

A Hymn in Praise of Wisdom: Chapter 28

Chapter 28 is a puzzlement. It is a beautiful poem, a tribute to wisdom, a human attribute more valuable than gold or silver. It begins:

> There is a mine for silver and a place where gold is
> refined . . . (28:1)

The poem goes on to pay tribute to the complicated process of mining silver and refining gold:

> They open a shaft far from where men live . . .
> No bird of prey knows the path to it,
> The falcon's eye has not gazed upon it . . .
> The lion has not crossed it.
> Man sets his hand against the flinty rock . . .
> He carves out channels through rock. (28:4, 7–9)

Then it gets to its main point:

> But where can wisdom be found?
> Where is the source of understanding? . . .
> It cannot be found in the land of the living.
> The Deep says, "It is not with me."
> The Sun says, "I do not have it." (28:12–14)

And then the climax:

> God understands the way to it, He knows its
>   place . . . .
> The fear of the Lord is wisdom,
> To shun evil is understanding. (28:23, 28)

This is all very lovely and probably true, but what is it doing here? Its connection to the problems of Job seems tenuous at best, and it is hard to understand its serene, peaceful tone as coming from the mouth of Job. Gordis offers the ingenious, if far-fetched, suggestion that it was written by the same gifted author as the rest of the book, was found among his papers, and "when by some scribal accident, the third cycle became gravely disorganized and a good part of the text was lost, the sheet containing the Hymn to Wisdom . . . was placed by some scribe in the concluding cycle." Joseph Koterski suggests that because we stand at a transitional moment in the book, chapter 28 might present an interlude, dropping a curtain between acts of the drama. Or perhaps it functions as a kind of Greek chorus, "a voice from the angelic council" mentioned in chapter 1, saying things beyond the capacity of any of the participants in the dialogue to say. It would be a moment of calm before the (literal) storm when God appears in a whirlwind, and its message would be that there is a source of wisdom in the universe beyond what even the finest human minds can comprehend. That would make it an appropriate preparation for God's appearance a few chapters later.

Job's Oath of Innocence: Chapters 29–31

The dialogue between Job and his would-be comforters, which has occupied the first two-thirds of the book, reaches its climax in a lengthy outpouring of lyrical poetry as beautiful and moving as anything in the Bible. When I teach the book of Job, when I reread it for my own pleasure, I can never refrain from reading these lines aloud in Hebrew, just to enjoy the language and rhythm. Job summons up what his life was like before it all fell apart, an eloquent reverie that also serves to assert one more time his piety and his innocence. For this chapter, I would turn to the translation done by the poet Stephen Mitchell, first published in 1979. This chapter of Job, above all others, calls for a poet's touch.

> If only I could return to the days when God was my
>   guardian;
> when his fire blazed above me and guided me in the
>   dark—
> to the days when I was in blossom and God was a
>   hedge around me
> when he hadn't yet deserted me
> and my children sat at my side.
>
> As I walked to the square of the city and took my seat
>   of honor,

Young men held their breath; old men rose to their
    feet;
Rich men stopped speaking and put their fingers to
    their lips. (29:2–5, 7–8)

The phrase "when I was in blossom" deserves some comment. The Hebrew is *y'mei horpi*, literally "in the winter of
my life." Pope translates it nicely as "the autumn of my
life." It may strike us as strange to speak of "the autumn of
[one's] life" as the best time. We tend to think of autumn/
winter as a time of decline and approaching death. When
Frank Sinatra sings, "It was a very good year," he is looking back wistfully to his youthful past from "the autumn of
my life." But Job, remember, lives in the Middle East, where
there are only two seasons to the year, not four. Winter for
him is not ice, snow, and trees bare of their leaves, as it is for
many of us. Winter is a time of abundant rainfall, grass and
flowers growing, rivers flowing and crops thriving. Summer
is the season of relentless heat and the disappearance of the
life-giving rain. To speak of "the winter of my life" as a time
of youthful vigor is like Shakespeare's Cleopatra speaking of
"My salad days, / When I was green in judgement."

Job continues, telling us why he was afforded great respect
by his neighbors:

> For I rescued the poor, the desperate,
> those who had nowhere to turn.
> I brought relief to the beggar
> and joy to the widow's heart . . .

> I served as eyes for the blind,
> hands and feet for the crippled . . .
> And I thought, "I will live many years,
> growing as old as a palm tree." (29:12–13, 15–16, 18)

That last line may be a deliberate echo of Psalm 92:12, "the righteous bloom like a date palm, they thrive like a cedar in Lebanon." Or it may just be that the image of a blessed old life being like a venerable tree was a common one in ancient Israel.

But then Job goes on to lament, in chapter 30, how everything changed:

> And now I am jeered at by streetboys,
> whose fathers I would have considered
> unfit to take care of my dogs . . .
> They snigger behind my back.
> They stand behind me and sneer. (30:1, 9)

To my ear, there is something touching about Job's sense of self being so dependent on what others think of him. His words speak of a time when a man's reputation was his most precious possession. Why should Job be so depressed when members of the lowest class of society sneer at him? Why does their opinion matter so much to him? I think of how some professional athletes wilt under the pressure of being booed by fans who don't have one one-hundredth of the athletic skills they do, while others respond to the challenge of proving the fans wrong, or of all the seventh graders cast into self-loathing because of a derogatory remark from a classmate whom they may not even like. It seems that our egos are so fragile, so vulnerable to the insults of others. When Job was prosperous, he took pride not so much in his achievements as in the respect those achievements engendered in others. When his situation changed for the worse, the pain of his losses was intensified by the realization that people he previously had no reason to take seriously were now openly mocking him. Some years ago, the social critic Lewis Mumford suggested that the mass production of mirrors in the sixteenth century had more of an effect on society than is generally appreciated. For the first time, people had an accurate idea of what they looked like. Before that, their self-image was defined largely by the respect or scorn they saw in the eyes of others. Job's remarks in chapters 29 and 30 seem to reflect an age when a person's sense of self-worth was less the product of a healthy ego and more the result of society's opinion of him, respecting a man not only for his wealth and fame but for his admirable personal qualities and civic involvement.

In chapter 29, Job reflected nostalgically on the happiest times of his life. In chapter 30, we saw him lament the fall from grace that robbed him of that happiness. We turn now to chapter 31, his last extended remarks and the last lines of dialogue between him and his visitors, and we find him taking the conversation in another direction entirely. (In what follows, I return to citing the JPS translation.)

I have covenanted with my eyes not to gaze on a
    maiden.
If ever my feet have strayed from their course,
My heart followed after my eyes and a stain sullied my
    hands,
May my wife grind for another . . . [the implication is
    clearly sexual]
Did I ever brush aside the case of my servants
When they made a complaint against me?
What then should I do when God arises, when He calls
    me to account?
Did I deny the poor their needs or let a widow pine
    away
While I ate my bread alone? . . .
I never saw an unclad wretch, a needy man without
    clothing,
Whose loins did not bless me as he warmed himself
With the shearings of my sheep . . .
Did I ever rejoice over my enemy's misfortune?
Did I thrill when evil befell him?
I never let my mouth sin by wishing his
    death . . . (31:1, 5, 7–10, 13–17, 19–20, 29–30)

Job's lengthy insistence not only on his innocence but on
his exemplary piety has been termed "the code of the Jewish
gentleman," despite its origin in the mouth of a non-Israelite
(but from the pen of an Israelite author). Not only has he

never taken something that did not belong to him, he never failed to share what he had with the needy. Not only has he never committed adultery, he has never looked lustfully even at an unmarried woman.

And then, finally,

> The words of Job are at an end. (31:40)

The Hebrew is impressively succinct: *Tamu div'rei Iyov.*

Why is Job saying all these things? The conventional understanding is that this is a final rebuttal to the insinuations of his friends that he must have done something seriously wrong; otherwise, why would a righteous God be punishing him? So where Eliphaz charged him with "exact[ing] pledges from your fellows without reason and leav[ing] them naked" (22:6), Job replies that not only did he never do that, he supplied clothing to the unclothed (31:19–20). Where Eliphaz accused him of denying food to the hungry and sending needy widows away empty-handed (27:7, 9), Job insists that he never ate without sharing his food with widows and orphans (31:16–17). To read chapter 31 as a point-by-point rebuttal of Eliphaz and the others is certainly plausible, but I think there is another answer, one that elevates Job's words from the level of charge and countercharge and defines chapter 31 as the turning point of the entire book, words that set the stage for the book's thunderous climax.

Imagine the following scenario: A neighbor entrusts some valuable property, cash or jewels, to you or asks you to keep an eye on some of his animals while he is traveling on business. Despite your best efforts, they are stolen. The thief cannot be identified, and the neighbor is not above suspecting that you may have taken them for yourself. How can you clear your name in such a way that the neighbor will have no grounds for continuing to suspect you? "Not guilty in the absence of evidence" is not enough for him, and you are going to have to go on with him living next door to you and looking strangely at you for the foreseeable future. According to the Torah (Exod. 22:6–8), you can swear an oath before God that you have not taken anything that was not rightfully yours. Your neighbor is obliged to concede that a person will not swear falsely before God, and if he has no evidence against you, he has to accept your innocence in the matter.

Biblical and post-biblical criminal law rest on the premise that there is a God who stands for justice and will not take kindly to people who cover up their wrongdoing by swearing falsely in His name. Taking God's name in vain (in an oath, not in an expletive) is forbidden by one of the Ten Commandments. God functions as the safety net that permits the courts to let a defendant go free in a case where the verdict is not clear, feeling that God will find a way to balance the scales rather than let someone get away with his crime. There is a term in rabbinic jurisprudence, "not guilty in the eyes of the court but culpable in the sight of Heaven." The Talmud tells of how a prominent sage, the president of the Sanhedrin, was walking in the outskirts of Jerusalem when he saw a man rush past as if he were running for his life, followed by another man carrying a large knife. The two run into a cave, there is a scream, and the second man emerges, his knife dripping blood. He sees the sage looking at him and says, "You probably think I did something terrible in there. Well, that's too bad. The evidence is all circumstantial; you didn't see me do anything. And even if you had, you are only a single witness, no matter how distinguished and presumably reliable you are, and two witnesses are required in a capital case." With a sneer, the man with the knife walks away. Before he has gone three paces, he is bitten by a snake and dies.

Whether or not we believe that story, it shows the degree to which biblical and post-biblical law alike presumed a horror of invoking God's name falsely, because God's judgment ultimately catches up with the person who does that. We in modern times are probably less certain that God won't let a criminal get away with his crime, but I would like to think we find something to admire in a society so uncomfortable at the prospect of an innocent man being convicted on the basis of circumstantial evidence or inaccurate eyewitness accounts that they would rather let guilty people go free and rely on God to balance the scales of justice.

What does this have to do with the book of Job? When we considered Job's oath of innocence in chapter 31, we said it could plausibly be read as a point-by-point rejoinder to Eliphaz's accusations in the opening lines of the third cycle, chapter 22. Job insists, You accuse me of ignoring the needs of the poor; I tell you I never ignored the needs of the poor. You claim I was deaf to the cries of widows and orphans; I insist I never turned them away empty-handed. But Job has had earlier opportunities to respond to Eliphaz's claims and he may well have seen Eliphaz's words, as we have suggested, as sarcasm: Do you expect God to present you with an inventory of all your transgressions?

I would like to suggest another way of understanding chapter 31. I see it as Job invoking the law found in chapter 22 of Exodus, swearing an oath to his innocence. (Job is not an Israelite, of course, and not bound by the Torah, but the author and his readers might well assume that God's standards of justice extend to all societies. We have seen this anomalous pattern in the book of Job before: gentile characters crafted by a Jewish author and displaying a Jewish sensibility. And we see it in contemporary times in an Arthur Miller play or a Jonathan Kellerman mystery novel.) Job is saying:

> [I swear] by God who deprived me of justice, by
>   Shaddai who has embittered my life . . .
> I persist in my righteousness. (27:2, 6)

> I saved the poor man who cried out, the orphan who
>   had no one to help him.
> I gladdened the heart of the widow . . . (29:12–13)

> I have covenanted with my eyes not to gaze on a
>   maiden. (31:1)

> I never saw an unclad wretch, a needy man without
>   clothing,

Whose loins did not bless me as he warmed himself
With the shearing of my sheep . . . (31:19–20)

As I read Job's last statement, he is saying, I have begged
and pleaded. I have proclaimed my innocence. I have asked
Why? But I received no answer from God. Now I will use this
one last, desperate tactic in my quarrel with God. No more
pleading, no more begging. I invoke God's own law against
Him. I hereby swear in the name of that same God who has
denied me justice but in whom I still believe that I am innocent of all possible charges. I swear by the Name of that God
that I have done nothing wrong. God, according to Your own
law, You are required to appear in court, to present evidence
against me or, by failing to do that, recognize me as innocent
and drop all charges.

And God appears.

"Then the Lord replied to Job out of a whirlwind" (38:1).
Job has found the magic words to compel God to answer him.
He has used the Torah's law of justice, designed to protect
the innocent person wrongly accused, against God Himself.
Summoned by the power of the Torah, YHWH (no longer
Elohim or Shaddai) prepares to explain Himself to Job.

But before we come to what God has to say from the
whirlwind, we have to deal with an interruption by a brash
young man named Elihu.

8

Elihu

Chapters 32–37

If the opening verses of chapter 32 are to be believed, Elihu son of Berachel is a brash young man who, passing by, overhears the conversation between Job and his visitors and is frustrated by the inability of Job's friends to do a better job of defending God. He interrupts them, with the requisite apology for disagreeing with his elders, and in six rather tedious chapters proceeds to tell them what they have overlooked.

> Then Elihu son of Berachel the Buzite, of the clan of Ram, was angry—angry at Job because he thought himself right against God. He was angry as well at his three friends because they could not find an answer and left God looking guilty. (32:2–3)

For that last phrase, JPS reads "but merely condemned Job." I am attracted to Pope's reading, "and left God looking guilty." Pope's version follows that of the classic Jewish

Bible commentator Rashi, who cites this as an instance of *tikkun sofrim*, a scribal change to protect God's honor by not including a line in Scripture suggesting that God might have been wrong.

Elihu continues (and I cannot help noticing that he takes more words to get around to his point and to make his point than any of the other speakers):

> I have but a few years while you are old,
> Therefore I was too awestruck and fearful to hold
>   forth among you.
> I thought, Let age speak, let advanced years declare
>   wisdom.
> But truly . . . it is not the aged who are wise.
> Therefore I say, Listen to me, I would also hold forth,
> For I am full of words. (32:6–7, 9–10, 17–18)

Having established his right, indeed his need, to speak, what does Elihu have to say? Does he emphasize his youth to suggest that he is offering the perspective of a younger generation? He claims first that God *does* explain Himself, both before and after He punishes us. One of His chief avenues of communication is through dreams.

> Why do you complain against Him
> That He does not reply to any of men's charges?
> For God speaks time and again though man does not
>   perceive it.
> In a dream, a night vision, when deep sleep falls on
>   men . . .

> He opens man's understanding, terrifies him with
>   warning
> To deter him from evil. (33:13–17)

The translation of that last line is Pope's, a good rendering of a difficult verse. Elihu seems to be saying that, when
we have nightmares, dreams of bad things happening to us,
that is God's way of warning us not to do something we
might be contemplating, lest we incur His disfavor. Then
Elihu adds a strange note in verse 23:

> Unless he have by him an angel, one out of a
>   thousand,
> To testify to his righteousness.

He seems to be alluding to some sort of guardian angel,
perhaps one of the divine beings mentioned in chapter 1
who functioned as God's council, who would intercede on
a person's behalf to elicit God's forgiveness. Even as God
has counselors like Satan to accuse humans of misbehavior,
He has others who function as "defense attorneys" on our
behalf. Maimonides, in his major philosophical-theological
work, *The Guide for the Perplexed*, has a brief discussion of
Job, and when he comes to Elihu and the guardian angel,
he explains it in this way: "When a man is ill to the point
of death, if an angel intercedes for him, his intervention is
accepted. . . . The invalid is saved and restored to the best
of states. However, this does not continue indefinitely, there
being no continuous intercession. It takes place only two or

three times" (*Guide*, book 3, chapter 23). Maimonides does not make it clear whether he personally believes this or is only explicating Elihu's enigmatic reference.

Job Betrays His Wickedness by Attributing Wickedness to God: Chapter 34

Elihu's second point is that Job proves his impiety by insisting on his innocence and, by implication, calling God unjust and untruthful. Only an arrogant man would speak of God that way.

> For Job has said, "I am right; God has deprived me of
>   justice.
> Concerning my case, He lies." (34:5–6)

(The Hebrew text reads "I lie," which makes no sense. The Septuagint, the first translation of the Bible into Greek, reads "He," and one suspects it is another case of a pious scribe changing a single word so as not to call God a liar.)

> What kind of man is Job,
> Who drinks mockery like water and makes common
>   cause with evildoers? . . .
> Men of understanding, listen to me.
> Far be it from God to do evil.
> He pays a man according to his actions . . .
> For God does not act wickedly,
> Shaddai does not pervert justice . . .

Does one call the king a scoundrel?
He has no set time for a man to appear before Him for
    judgment. (34:5–6, 10–12, 18, 23)

In other words, God gets around to everyone sooner or
later, for good or ill, and it is not for us to judge Him. He
will judge us.

In chapter 35, Elihu briefly makes the point that God does
not profit from our righteousness, nor is He harmed by our
wrongdoing. He rewards and punishes because of His dedi-
cation to goodness.

If you sin, what do you do to Him?
If you are righteous, what do you give Him? (35:6–7)

Chapters 36 and 37 are basically an extended assertion
that God does indeed punish those who do wrong and protect those who do right. At one point, Elihu suggests that
sometimes God inflicts suffering on innocent people to
impel them to ask "What might I have done to deserve this?"
and examine their lives more closely. People are made better
through their suffering. It inoculates them against the danger of self-righteousness and imbues them with a sense of
kinship with fellow sufferers. There is something "unripe"
about the person who has never tasted disappointment or
sorrow. Alter captures this nuance in his translation of 36:15:

He frees the afflicted through their affliction
And through oppression, He lays bare their ear.

This sounds more than a little like the point we saw C. S. Lewis making, describing pain as "God's chisel to perfect us," as we discussed in chapter 7. And perhaps there is a case to be made for it. Suffering may not be pleasant to endure, but might it somehow be good for our spiritual growth, ridding us of an unrealistic confidence? In an article in the *Harvard Divinity Bulletin* (Winter–Spring 2011), a religiously sympathetic psychologist sees how this approach to suffering might in fact be superior to the average therapist's inclination to ease the person's pain rather than make him work through it. James Davies writes, "The positive model [of suffering, as contrasted with the therapeutic effort that sees it negatively] holds that suffering can have a redemptive role to play in human life, that from affliction there can be derived some unexpected gains. . . . The positive vision thus considered sees suffering as a kind of liminal region through which we can pass from a worse to a better place. Or alternatively, suffering [can be seen as] a natural outcome of confronting certain unpleasant facts about the human and natural world, facts we may well need to confront if we are to live more firmly rooted in reality." Dr. Davies quotes Psalm 119:71: "It has been good for me that I was afflicted, that I might be well instructed and learn Thy holy laws."

Elihu concludes his extended interruption with a tribute to the awesome majesty of God, as made manifest in a thunder-and-lightning storm.

What are we to make of Elihu? Medieval scholars, committed as they were to seeing the Bible as a perfect book dictated by a perfect God, had no choice but to see these chapters as an extension of the friends' argument. If the author of the book saw fit to offer these insights as the last words of the dialogue, he must have considered them the strongest arguments one could make from the perspective of the defenders of God's honor. Though it is never explicitly stated, these pre-modern sages must have believed that the author's sympathies lay with the friends who made the case for God, not with Job who questioned Him. The traditional commentators see Elihu as he presented himself, another defender of God with compelling arguments overlooked by the three who spoke before him. Maimonides goes so far as to call Elihu "the most perfect among them in knowledge."

Modern critics, by contrast, are virtually unanimous in seeing the Elihu chapters as an interpolation by another hand. Like the producers who added happy endings to Shakespearean tragedies, like the Yiddish translations of classics made available to Jewish immigrants in the early twentieth century that bore the words on their title page *ubersetzt und verbessert*, "translated and improved," it would seem that some reader of the book of Job early in its history of transmission was provoked to think, *Had I been there, I could have made a more persuasive case on God's behalf*, and to make sure that no future readers would be misled by the inadequate arguments of Eliphaz, Bildad, and Zophar, he added his thoughts to the biblical text.

Gordis makes an effort to defend the unity of authorship, despite glaring differences of style and diction, by suggest-

ing that the original author of Job, years later, had thoughts
he wished he had put into his original composition. (I have
often felt that way about a speech I gave or an article I wrote,
coming up sometime afterward with insights I wish I might
have had sooner. The phenomenon is often referred to as
l'esprit d'escalier, "the clever remark that occurs to one on
the staircase as one is leaving a gathering.") So the original
author went back and added the character of Elihu, putting
those late thoughts into his mouth. As to the unmistak-
able difference of style, Gordis cites the examples of Shakespeare's writings as they evolved from the early romantic
comedies to the verbal extravagance of *The Tempest* and *King
Lear,* or Goethe returning in his old age to add the surreal
part 2 to the more conventional part 1 of *Faust.*

Most contemporary scholars tend to dismiss the Elihu
chapters as the work of another hand and to regard them as
inferior to the rest of the book. Ginsberg calls him "Elihu
the intruder," dismissing his orations as "turgid and long-
winded" and writing that "the effort required to understand
the Elihu speeches is all out of proportion to the profundity
of thought." For Alter, "the plausible consensus is that it is
an interpolation, the work of another poet. . . . The poetry
he speaks is by and large not up to the level of the poetry
of the debate . . . and there is a whole series of Hebrew
terms that appear only in the Elihu speeches." Pope agrees
with those who dismiss the Elihu chapters as "having scant
value either as literature or as a solution to the problem of
evil. Their style is diffuse and pretentious [and] Elihu is

completely ignored in the Epilogue when God rebukes Job's comforters." As we have seen, there may be one idea found in his utterances that deserves our contemplation. Despite that, I am inclined to see it as a foreign element that does not stem from either the Fable of Job or the Poem as its author wrote it.

But even as I reject Elihu's theology and am unimpressed by his rhetoric, I endorse his effort. To me, he is not being critical of the biblical author. (What's the matter with you? Is that the best case you can make for God?) He is accepting the author's tacit invitation to join in the discussion, as every reader of Job must be tempted to join in the discussion rather than just read it. A good book tells a story, and the reader is either pleased or displeased, intrigued or bored. A great book invites the reader to respond, to argue, to challenge. In a sense, Elihu is doing what I have been doing, what Judy Klitsner does in *Subversive Sequels in the Bible*, what rabbis and ministers do on a weekly basis in their sermons: not disagreeing with a biblical or rabbinic text but wrestling with it. With Elihu's intervention recognized for the late interpolation I believe it is, the book of Job begins to resemble classical Jewish texts like the Talmud or those volumes of Torah with commentary, in which the basic text is surrounded by a number of commentators and commentators on the commentators, responding to the text and to what others have said about it.

The arguments against the Elihu passages being an integral part of the book rest on matters of style ("turgid and long-winded") and content (he adds very little that is new and significant). Then there is the inherent implausibility of the impassioned arguments of chapters 3–31 being accessible to eavesdropping by a casual bystander. Beyond that, he has a specifically Israelite name after the author of Job has gone to great lengths to present Job's case as a universal issue, not a specifically Israelite one. But to me, there is another, even more compelling reason not to see these passages as part of the original book. They come between chapter 31 and chapter 38. As suggested, I see Job's oath of innocence in chapter 31 and God's speech from the whirlwind in chapters 38–41 as being inextricably linked. Indeed, I see them as the key to understanding what the author of Job was trying to say. Most annoying of all, the Elihu interruptions keep us from hearing what God has to say to Job when He finally deigns to answer him.

9

Out of the Whirlwind

Then the Lord answered Job out of the whirlwind
saying,
Who is this who darkens counsel, speaking without
knowledge?
Gird your loins like a man,
I will ask and you will answer Me. (38:1–3)

(JPS translates *s'arah* as "tempest," which is accurate, but I am persuaded by Alter's comment: "The phrase 'the Voice from the Whirlwind' has been so deeply embedded in the imagination of spoken English after the King James translation that it seems wise not to tamper with it.")

The tone of the narrative becomes markedly different for the last four chapters of the book, maybe because it is God speaking and we expect God to sound different than Eliphaz or Elihu, maybe because the book is racing toward its climax. We note several things about God's opening words to Job. The first is the use of God's personal Name, YHWH, for the first time since the author of the Poem took over from the Fable in chapter 3 (except for 12:9, which is almost certainly a scribal error). As I've said, YHWH is God's intimate Name, shared only with those who are, so to speak, on a first-name basis with Him. It is the name God revealed to Moses at the Burning Bush, the first step toward liberating Israel from slavery (Exod. 6:2–3). If that represented the first step toward freeing the slaves and bringing them into a new relationship with a Redeemer God, the use of that name in the opening words from the whirlwind may presage God's forging a new, deeper relationship with Job. When Job and his friends *talk about* God, they use more abstract terms—El, Elohim, Shaddai. But when Job actually *encounters* God, the relationship is a more personal one. No longer an object of theological conjecture and debate, God has become an awesomely real presence.

Martin Buber distinguishes between theology, the intellectual contemplation of the nature of God, and religion, the life-altering experience of actually being in the presence of God. The difference between them, one explicator of Buber has suggested, is like the difference between reading a menu and having dinner. Theology can inform and enlighten, but only religion can nourish us. For thirty-five chapters, Job and his friends have been concerned with theology. With God's appearance out of the whirlwind, the narrative turns to religion.

The author of the Twenty-third Psalm makes a similar point. When all is going smoothly in his life, surrounded by green pastures and still waters, the psalmist talks *about* God, referring to God as He. But when he finds himself for the first time in the valley of the shadow of death and discovers that God has not abandoned him, only then does he say for the first time, "for *Thou* art with me."

The second thing we note in the opening lines of God's speech is that God has not come down to earth to explain Himself or answer Job's questions. God's first words are, in effect, I'll ask the questions around here. "I will ask and you will answer Me" (38:3). And His first question is:

> Where were you when I laid the earth's foundations?
> Speak, if you have understanding.
> Do you know who fixed its dimensions
> Or measured it with a line?
> Onto what were its bases sunk? Who set its
>   cornerstone? (38:4–6)

The point God is making is that, in Pope's formulation, "God does not need the help or advice of impatient and ignorant mortals to control the world any more than He needed them to create it."

The voice from the whirlwind continues:

> Who closed the Sea behind doors when it gushed forth
>   out of the womb . . .
> When I made breakers My limit for it . . .
> And said, "You may come so far and not further.
> Here your surging waves will stop?" (38:8, 10–11)

The emphasis on the sea in that passage is not arbitrary. It would seem that ancient peoples, especially those living within sight of the Mediterranean or some other ocean, had an innate ancestral memory of a time when the earth was covered by water, as described in chapter 1 of Genesis and in the story of Noah. When they saw the tide encroach on the dry land, creeping ever closer, it may have awakened fears that the ocean waters were coming back to reclaim what had once been theirs. (I am writing these lines shortly after high winds and waves drove the waters of the North Atlantic to spill over seawalls and destroy oceanfront homes in communities north of Boston, and in a week when unprecedented floods inundated much of Australia. I visited New Orleans shortly after Hurricane Katrina and saw how entire neighborhoods were washed away by a combination of hurricane-driven winds and the overflowing of Lake Pontchartrain. And since then, we have seen the damage wrought by the tsunami that struck Japan in the winter of 2011. The nightmares of our ancestors may not have been as paranoid as they might appear.)

To the ancients, one of God's major responsibilities was to set limits to the sea's encroachment onto the dry land, saying to the waters, "Thus far you may come and no further." More than one ancient society's religious celebrations included commemorating the victory of their god, representing safety and security, over the forces of chaos as represented by the sea, standing for destruction and danger. We saw a trace of this in 7:12, where Job pleaded, "Am I the Sea or the Sea Monster that You have set a watch over me?"

A similar thought, that it is a sign of God's might that He keeps the ocean within bounds so that it cannot reclaim the dry land, is found in Jeremiah 5:22:

> Shall you not revere Me? says the Lord . . .
> Who set the sand as a boundary to the sea,
> As a limit for all time, not to be transgressed?
> Though its waves toss, they cannot prevail.
> Though they roar, they cannot pass it.

God's opening lines are an impressive articulation of His power, but Job never challenged His power. It was God's commitment to justice and mercy that Job has repeatedly called into question. So God, without in any way conceding that He is answering Job's charges, here adds a note of benevolence to His boast of creation: The world not only exists thanks to God. It is designed to make life possible, even pleasant.

> Who cut a channel for the torrents and a path for the
>   thunderstorm,
> To rain down on the uninhabited land, on the
>   wilderness where no man is? . . .
> Can you send up an order to the clouds
> For an abundance of water to cover you?
> Can you dispatch the lightning on a mission and have
>   it answer you, "I am ready"? (38:25–26, 34–35)

Conspicuous by its absence in that passage and in the lines that follow is any reference to human beings, as if God were saying to Job, It's not all about you. You are not the center of My universe. God sends rain on the farmer's fields so that the crops will grow and people will have food to eat. But He also sends rain to desolate corners of the earth where there are no farmers, no fields, and no crops. God has an entire universe to care for, and Job is only a small part of it.

There is a strong commitment in the Hebrew Bible and in post-biblical thought to the idea that the world was created for the sake of humanity, sometimes even that it was created for the sake of the Jewish people. Human beings, fashioned in the image of God, sharing with God a sense of right and wrong, were the crown of Creation. God tells the first humans, "Fill the earth and master it. Rule the fish of the sea, the birds of the sky and all the living things that creep on the earth" (Gen. 1:28). No wonder we whose worldview has been shaped by the Bible feel betrayed when things don't work out to our satisfaction. But God seems to be saying here that a world designed exclusively for the benefit of humans was our vision, not His.

God then proceeds, in the last verses of chapter 38 and in chapter 39, with an extended description of the animal kingdom, including both farm animals that are useful to man and exotic wild animals that are of no practical benefit to human beings. Here God seems to be reinforcing the point "it's not all about you." The poetry is often eloquent and imaginative.

Can you hunt prey for the lion? . . .
Do you know the season when the mountain goats
    give birth?
Their young are healthy, they grow up in the open,
They leave and return no more . . .
Who sets the wild ass free, who loosens the bonds of
    the onager?
The wings of the ostrich beat joyously;
Are her pinions and plumage like the stork's? . . .
Do you give the horse his strength?
He paws with force, he charges into battle.
He scoffs at fear, he cannot be frightened. . . .
Does the eagle soar at your command,
Building his nest high, dwelling in the rock? (38:39,
    39:1, 4–5, 13, 19, 21–22, 26–27)

Having reminded Job that He created the world, a feat beyond the capacity of the most powerful human being, that He designed it so that it would be livable, providing rain and snow, setting limits to the encroachment of the seas, and that He populated it with a panoply of both useful and exotic creatures, God, as it were, pauses for breath, challenging Job:

Will the contender with Shaddai yield?
He who reproves God, let him answer for it.
And Job answered the Lord, saying:
Lo, I am small; how can I answer You?
My hand I lay on my mouth.

I have spoken once, I will not reply.
Twice, but I will say no more. (40:1–5)

The gesture of laying one's hand on one's mouth seems to be a way of acknowledging that one is in the presence of someone so much greater and more worthy of respect that it would be presumptuous to speak in his presence. Job used the phrase in 29:9, remembering how people used to respect him.

Is Job persuaded, or is he only intimidated? Has God answered his complaints or only cowed him into withdrawing them? Chapters 38 and 39 are an eloquent tribute to God's power, but God's power was never the issue. Everyone—Job, Eliphaz, Bildad, Zophar, even Elihu—acknowledged God's awesome power. It was His fairness and kindness that were at issue. Would God let things happen to people that they did not deserve because He was not constrained by considerations of fairness or people's unhappiness? Throughout the book, Job's lament has been, What can I do? It's His world and He can do what He wishes with it. But I was hoping that He would treat good people kindly. Is this the answer of the book of Job? God saying, You accuse Me of being a bully? I'll show you what I do to people who accuse Me of being a bully!

Were the book to end at this point, with Job cowed into submission, we would come away from it disappointed in the author's conclusion. To have written this magnificent poem, only to have it end on a note of "Yes, the world is unfair but what can we do about it?" would be unsatisfying. But God is not finished. To this point, the words the author has put into God's mouth have been clear and compelling, if somewhat irrelevant to Job's complaint. (God seems to be saying, I'll set the agenda here, if you please.)

God's final remarks, in chapters 40 and 41, are strikingly different. God describes two animals—they may be real, they may be mythical—who are not only exotic and of no benefit to man, like the ostrich and the eagle, but are ferocious and dangerous. One is Behemoth (from the Hebrew *behemah*, "beast"), maybe a bull, maybe a hippopotamus; the other is Leviathan, maybe a crocodile. I am surprised by the number of critics who see chapter 40 as a reprise and extension of chapter 39. Just as God, in His creative abundance, fashioned creatures like the eagle and ostrich that are of no use to man, so He fashioned creatures like the hippo and the crocodile that are ugly and dangerous by human standards, to make the point that He is not bound by human standards of aesthetics or security. I disagree, siding with the critics who find a different message in chapter 40 than we found in chapter 39. I think there is a reason why chapter 40 begins by repeating God's challenge to Job and Job's mini-apology, his confession of inadequacy. God's comments are about to move to a different level, and the answer to Job's question, Why do good people suffer in God's world?, will begin to emerge.

I agree with Alter when he writes that this is not just another example of God's bountiful zoological creativity. "In his daunting proportions, his fierce vitality and his absolute impregnability, he represents a mythological heightening of the actual beast, just as Leviathan is even more patently a mythological heightening of the Egyptian crocodile." I would extend Alter's point. To me, Behemoth and Leviathan represent forces of the created world with which even God Himself is challenged to contend. They are necessary dimensions of God's world; that is why He created them. But even God has to exert Himself to keep them from getting out of hand. (The clear implication to Job: Could you do a better job of it? "Then would I praise you for the triumph your right hand has achieved" [40:14].)

Consider the language:

Take now Behemoth whom I made as I made you,
His strength is in his loins, his might in the muscles
of his belly.
He makes his tail [a euphemism for the male sexual
organ] stand up like a cedar . . .
Only his Maker can draw the sword against him . . .
Can anyone capture him while he is looking? (40:15–17,
19, 24)

(The last line is my attempt to make sense of a difficult verse. JPS reads "can he be taken by his eyes.")

Leviathan is a more familiar monster, well attested to in Canaanite and Ugaritic mythology. Known there as Lotan the Sea Monster, he was the foe whom the Canaanite god of creation had to defeat in order to create the world. After an epic struggle, he succeeded in slaying Lotan and used half of his carcass as the foundation of the world and the other half to hold up the heavens. As the Canaanite myth would have it, the god's victory over Leviathan was a near thing, a struggle in which the god had to exert himself to the utmost to prevail. That this tradition was well-known in Israel is attested to by such texts as Psalm 74:13–14:

> It was You who drove back the Sea with Your might,
> It was You who crushed the heads of Leviathan.

Or Isaiah 26:21–25:

> The Lord shall come forth from His place
> To punish the dwellers of the earth for their iniquity.
> In that day, the Lord will punish with His cruel and
>   mighty sword
> Leviathan the Elusive Serpent.
> He will slay the Dragon of the Sea.

But perhaps the most significant biblical reference to the epic struggle between the Creator-God and the Sea Monster is a verse that does not mention Leviathan at all, Genesis 1:20–21:

> And God said, Let the waters bring forth swarms of
>   living creatures, and birds that fly above the earth.
>   God created the great sea monsters and all the
>   living creatures of every kind.

The canonical Israelite account of Creation in Genesis 1 pictures God fashioning Leviathan without a semblance of struggle. It was just one more item on His to-do list for day 5.

Chapter 40 of Job tells a different story. Here, controlling Leviathan is a challenge even for God.

> Can you draw out Leviathan with a fishhook?
> Can you press down his tongue with a rope?
> Can you put a ring through his nose? . . .
> Will he make an agreement with you to be taken as
>   your slave?
> [Dare to] lay a hand on him and you will never think
>   of battle again. (40:25–26, 28, 32)

(I take the last line to mean "Just try to capture him; that will be the end of your career as a soldier-hunter.")

Chapter 41, essentially the last chapter of the dialogue between God and Job, continues in the same vein. The number of verses dedicated to describing Leviathan would seem to reflect the creature's importance in what God has to say to Job.

> See, any hope [of taming him] must be disappointed;
> One is prostrated by the very sight of him.
> [His boast is:] "Who then can stand up to me?
>   Whoever confronts me, I will requite."
> Divine beings are in dread as he rears up; as he
>   crashed down, they cringe.

No sword that overtakes him can prevail . . .

No arrow can put him to flight. (41:1–3, 17–18, 20)

Those are God's last words from the whirlwind. What is He saying? In chapters 38–39, I hear God saying, What gives you the idea that you and I are on equal footing, like two neighbors settling a dispute? I created the world and everything in it. But I didn't stop there. I made sure the world would remain a livable place, sending the rain so that crops would grow. I arrange for a variety of animals to know when it is their mating season, to perpetuate the species. Then God pauses, and Job admits that he is overmatched and overwhelmed.

Had the speech from the whirlwind ended there, had the book essentially ended there, God would have intimidated Job into withdrawing his challenge ("Son, you don't want to mess with Me"), but would not have answered his question. That is why chapters 40 and 41 are so essential. In these passages, I find God saying, I didn't simply create a world that would run by itself. It was a world that depended on My constant involvement and intervention. Behold Behemoth and Leviathan, My creatures. They are responsible for most of the misery in the world, most of the bad things that happen to people (like you) who deserve better. But I need them in order to bring about the kind of world I had in mind when I created it. Behemoth is the Primal Life Force that gives people the energy to do things and to have an impact on the lives of other people for good or ill. Thousands of years from now, a man named Sigmund Freud will call it Id and Eros. Part of it is sexual. That is the significance of the priapic male organ referred to in 40:16. That part of it is probably responsible for more happiness and more pain, more joy and more anguish, than anything else in My universe. But would you prefer a world without love, without the drive to find that one special person who makes you complete, restoring the wholeness that existed in the Garden of Eden, a man and a woman coming together to "become one flesh"? Without Eros, life would not replenish itself. For all the problems it causes, for all the grief it generates, a world without Eros would be a world without love, a world without children, a world deprived of the motivation to make things better for future generations.

Part of Behemoth is the acquisitive instinct, the drive to do things better and have more of the good things in life than other people do. He is capable of provoking much creativity, much accomplishment, and many plagues, crime, fraud, and envy, but without that selfish-erotic-acquisitive instinct, how would humans ever improve on the world they found? Why would they create families, establish businesses, invent things, write books, and fashion works of art? There is a Talmudic legend cited in chapter 5 about the day people trapped the impulse for selfishness, only to discover that life could not go on without it. Part of this dangerous but essential power, one of the things that make human beings unique among God's creatures, is the ability to impose choice on instinct. As far as we know, no other living creature can do

that. Animals can learn to avoid things that lead to bad outcomes. They can master complicated ways of getting food.
But an animal cannot *choose* to go hungry. It cannot choose
to disregard a female in heat during the mating season. Only
humans can employ conscience, will, and a sense of right
and wrong to supersede instinct. Lust, greed, and hunger
are powerful forces, but God's world needs them, and God
has given us the ability to control them.

In order to have goodness freely chosen (and if it's not
freely chosen, can we call it good?), there has to be the possibility of choosing evil, choosing to harm, to destroy. We can
ask, Why didn't God prevent the Holocaust? Why couldn't
He arrange for Hitler to be run over by a streetcar in 1920
and thereby save millions of lives? That's not His job, to
stage-manage people's lives and take away their responsibility for being good. Before we ask, Where was God?, I would
ask, Why did so many people vote for Hitler? I would ask,
Why did so many people look the other way when he began
to victimize their neighbors? Without Behemoth, without
that freedom to act selfishly and choose wrongdoing, you
might have obedience, but not goodness. Behemoth can
manifest himself in the tendency of people to get angry, and
that can have tragic results, from domestic violence to inci-
dents of road rage to murders and even war. But without
that capacity for anger, would people have fought a civil war
to end slavery? Would their protests have made child labor
illegal and struck down racial segregation? Would a nation
have mobilized to go to war to fight Hitler? From time to

time, Behemoth can get out of hand, and that is when God has to intervene to clean up the mess, motivating people to set limits to Id even as He set limits to the sea. But you would not want to have to deal with Behemoth on your own, without God's inspiration.

And Leviathan, the agent of chaos? What role does he play in God's scheme? The biblical account of Creation is the story of God imposing order where there had been chaos, separating light from darkness, water from dry land, plant from plant and species from species, so that apple trees would yield apples and no other fruit, and cats would give birth to kittens, never puppies. But by nightfall on the sixth day, a residue of chaos seems to have remained. Leviathan was tamed but not eliminated. And that chaos, that element of sheer chance, continues to play a role in God's world. A man just misses his train. Maybe he takes the next one and meets the woman he will marry. Or maybe he is late for his meeting and a competitor gets the contract instead of him. A ground ball hits a pebble and one team wins the World Series instead of the other. God's will? Only insofar as God arranged for the race not to be always to the swift and for time and chance to enter into all things (Eccles. 9:11–12).

Newsom writes that God describes Behemoth and Leviathan "with evident admiration." Unlike the message we find in Genesis 1, chaos seems to be as much a part of God's plan for the world as order is. The engine that drove, and continues to drive, evolution has been the spontaneous emergence of random genetic traits that give some people an advantage over others. By sheer chance, some people were born with better eyesight and faster reflexes than others. They became better hunters and providers (and in today's world, highly paid athletes), were more attractive marriage partners, and produced more children, many of whom inherited their genetic blessings. Some people, by chance, were born healthier or more intelligent than others, enabling them to live longer and better lives, produce more children, and, over time, contribute to a healthier, brighter population. Was that unfair on God's part? It was totally unfair to those left behind, to the genetically cheated, but that seems to have been God's plan for an ever-improving human race: bless some arbitrarily and stand prepared to sustain the others in spirit. If that offends your sense of justice, the response should be not to rail against God but to work for a society that sustains the afflicted, the disabled, the less well-endowed, so that they too can live meaningful lives. And where will the energy to do that come from if not from a God who cares about all His creatures?

But, as God warned Job, Leviathan, like Behemoth, can get out of hand. Natural disasters, earthquakes, floods, and droughts are not really random though they may be unexpected. But they are chaotic in the sense that they are unpredictable and serve no human purpose. Natural laws are blind to considerations of good and bad. Forest fires may be Nature's way of clearing out old growth to make room for new, but when expanding populations lead to building new homes near old forests, the results, however much in conformity with natural law, may be tragic. Genetic anomalies can be a curse as readily as they can be a blessing, as our family learned, and sometimes they can be both. For example, it seems that some people living in Africa millions of years ago were born less vulnerable to the threat of malaria. They lived longer and had more children to inherit that immunity. But that immunity, like so many gifts, came with a cost; today many people whose family trees go back to Africa but who live in countries where malaria is not a problem find themselves vulnerable to sickle-cell anemia. Genetic roulette, one form of chaos, has its costs as well as its benefits. That is why God and we are engaged in an ongoing struggle with Leviathan, to identify and take advantage of the beneficial accidents of birth and minimize the harmful ones. I see doctors and researchers who work with the victims of genetic accidents as doing God's work, encouraged and inspired by God as they struggle with Leviathan. I see rescue workers in the aftermath of a flood or earthquake doing God's work, restoring order where chaos has struck rather than justifying the disaster as the outcome of God's inscrutable will. In the gift shop of a Japanese garden park in Florida, I spied a T-shirt that read "Chaos = the constant unfolding of the absurd, Life itself."

The last half of God's speech would seem to be an admission that the world is not perfect, but not because of any weakness or limitation on God's part. Our world could not be the world that God had in mind if it did not include Behemoth and Leviathan, ambition and randomness, and all the harm they can cause. God's world was not perfect at the end of the week of Creation, it was not perfect during the time of the Bible, and it is not perfect in the twenty-first century, when some babies are still born genetically impaired and people still have trouble controlling their greed, lust, and anger. God's world is not perfect because "perfect" means "finished," as it does when we speak of the "perfect tense" in grammar to describe an action that is over. God's creative process is still going on.

God is not apologizing to Job in His speech from the whirlwind. There is not a trace of "you were right and I was wrong." God is patiently explaining that goodness freely chosen cannot occur without the freedom to choose evil, deceit, and selfishness. He is pointing out that even an omnipotent God cannot answer all prayers, even when offered by people who deserve to have their prayers answered. God cannot simultaneously answer the pious farmer's prayer for rain and the charitable vacationer's prayer for sunshine, the home team's fans' prayer for victory and the visiting team's fans' prayers for an upset.

God has taken the extraordinary step of personally responding to a human being's challenge because Job, having suffered more than most of us and deserving it less, merited an answer and because Job used the norms of the Torah to summon Him. Now God has said what He had to say. If we set aside the end of chapter 42, the concluding lines of the Fable, in which He chastens the friends and restores Job's fortune, God has finished.

Job says two things, preceded by a brief apology, at the beginning of chapter 42, and they are crucial to understanding the book. Here, more than anywhere else, one gets the sense that he is speaking for the author.

> Job said in reply to the Lord:
> I know that You can do everything, that no plan is
>   impossible for You.
> "Who is this who obscures counsel without
>   knowledge?"
> Indeed I spoke without understanding.
> Of things beyond me, which I did not know. (42:1–3)

That is the apology. As one scholar puts it, "What God said about the ocean (38:11) applies to Man's understanding of God as well: Thus far shall you go and no further." Then Job spells out what he has learned and come to believe about God:

> I had heard [about] You with my ears,
> But now I see you with my eyes. (42:5)

That is, until now Job's understanding of God has been strictly theological, based on what learned people had taught him, and he had problems reconciling those teachings with the facts of his life and the lives of others he cared about. But now he has met God, and meeting God is very different from being taught about God. For a human being to claim that he understands God would be to assert his superiority over the divine, as if to say, God is the subject and I am the authority on that subject. Using Buber's typology, Job has evolved from the realm of theology to that of religious experience, from discussing God to encountering God. Job's questions have been answered, his doubts erased not by the *content* of God's words from the whirlwind but by the *contact*. He has met God and all theological quibbles have melted away.

Then Job concludes his response, and the author of the book of Job concludes his masterpiece, with seven words of Hebrew that seem to me to be the key to understanding the book and that are, alas, untranslatable with any degree of certainty:

Al ken em'as v'nihamti al afar v'efer. (42:6)

The translation offered by JPS reads, "Therefore I recant and relent, being but dust and ashes." In other words, God, forgive me, a mere mortal, for having doubted You. The King James translation renders it, "Wherefore I abhor myself and repent in dust and ashes." The Revised Standard Version understands it in a similar vein: "Therefore I despise myself and repent in dust and ashes." I have problems with those renditions. First of all, the phrase "dust and ashes" never refers to a location, to a person finding himself in the midst of actual dirt. It is always, without exception, a synonym for human frailty and mortality. (JPS gets that right.) There is no Hebrew antecedent for the word "myself" as the object of Job's despising. The object has to be inferred. Here we see one last time how theology determines interpretation. Instead of learning about Job and God from the text, we read our presuppositions *into* the text. Those whose religious outlook is rooted in the doctrine of Original Sin find in these difficult words a confession of Job's worthlessness and his presumptuousness in challenging God. For both of those traditional, theologically driven translations, the ending of the Poem has Job admitting that God was right and Job was a sinner for doubting Him. I find it hard to believe that the author of the Poem means to portray Job as the villain of the story.

Job's last line has to be more than a repetition of the apology he offered in 40:4–5. Otherwise, why did the author feel the need to add the Behemoth and Leviathan passages? Half of that last line is intelligible enough. *Al ken* means "therefore" and *afar v'efer* literally means "dust and ashes." It is a recognizable biblical phrase signifying insignificance. Job used the phrase in 30:19 to convey his fallen state, and Abraham uses it to characterize his unworthiness when he argues with God on behalf of the people of Sodom (Gen. 18:27). But it is the two verbs that baffle us. It is not that they are obscure words, like so much of the vocabulary in Job. On the contrary, they are quite familiar. The problem is that they can refer to several different things.

I consulted my biblical dictionary, the redoubtable *Brown-Driver-Briggs Hebrew and English Lexicon of the Old Testament.* For *em'as* (from the root *ma'os*), it offers: to refuse, to reject, to deem worthless. That might fit the traditional interpretation, but it can as readily lead us in another direction. What is it that Job is rejecting? We will have to find the key to understanding Job's conclusion in the second verb. For *nihamti* (from the root *nahem*), the lexicon suggests: to be sorry, to console oneself, to have compassion for others, to repent for what one has done (this is the nuance that the King James picks up), and to be comforted.

The most extreme and least plausible interpretation I know of takes *em'as* in the sense of "reject" and *nihamti* as a variation of *rihamti*, "to pity." It takes the verse to mean, If that is the kind of God you are, I reject You and I feel sorry for human beings. That may be the theology of the scholar who proposed it and it does fit the Hebrew, but I can't believe that is the conclusion the author wants to leave us with.

Another scholar, aware that the most common meaning of *nahem* is "to comfort," translates the climactic verse of the book, "I despise [my suffering] and I seek comfort [in having met God] though I am but dust and ashes." That strikes me as more plausible than some, but not quite there.

The poet and scholar Stephen Mitchell, who is a superb Hebraist, challenges the King James/Revised Standard rendering of the verse on linguistic as well as theological grounds. Not only are they rooted in a theory of Man as a depraved sinner who has no right to challenge God, they misunderstand the Hebrew terminology in the process.

Mitchell takes the first half of the verse to mean "Therefore I consider worthless [everything I have said to this point]." It is Job's uninformed arguments, not Job himself, that deserve to be rejected. Then, for the second half of the line, Mitchell notes that the verb *nahem* is used ten times in the book of Job, and in every one of them without exception, it means "to comfort or console," never "to repent."

> This would be my consolation. (6:10)
> When I think my bed will comfort me . . . (7:13)
> You are all mischievous comforters. (16:2)
> Why do you offer me empty consolation? (21:34)

He translates that last line, "I am comforted about being mortal."

My own understanding of this crucial verse largely follows Mitchell. It would read, "I reject [everything that has been said to this point by me and my visitors] and [having met God and been reassured that I am not alone and abandoned in this world] I am comforted, vulnerable human being that I am."

On that note, the Poem of Job ends. The biblical book of Job adds the happy ending that once brought a close to the Fable. After the soaring eloquence of God's words from the whirlwind, the simplemindedness of this ending (Here you are, Job: more wealth, more children) strikes us as an anticlimax and leaves us puzzled as to why God would rebuke the three friends who had defended Him and affirm Job who had challenged Him. Clearly whoever put those words in God's mouth was unfamiliar with the Poem.

We have come to the end of our study of Job. What does it all mean? Why do good people suffer in a world ruled by God? There is no shortage of interpretations among those who have devoted themselves to this book.

10

Answers

The sages tell us, "God is like a mirror. The mirror never changes, but everyone who looks at it sees a different face." Some people read the book of Job and find that it confirms what they already want to believe. In effect, they find their own face looking back at them. But then there are readers who approach Job with an open mind, hoping to see something in the mirror that they have never seen before, something that will lead them to a new understanding. If we read the arguments of Eliphaz, Bildad, and Zophar without bias, we cannot dismiss them casually. Human beings *are* prone to deny or rationalize their misdeeds. God's calculations may very well not follow the rules of human logic. Then we read Job's responses, verging at times on blasphemy, and when we recall the circumstances out of which he has been speaking, however firm our faith in God may be, we find it hard not to sympathize with him. In the end, every one of us reads his own book of Job, colored by our own faith and personal history. But if we read it honestly, we will not be the same people when we come to the end of the book that we were when we began. At the very least, we will have to say, "I never thought of it that way before."

I set high standards for what I would consider a satisfactory answer to Job's problem, the problem of good people suffering in a world under God's control. First, it must assume the innocence of the victim. He need not be perfect, but in a just world, he should not deserve what happened to him. I will not consider the claim, often made in the name of religion, that since none of us is perfect, we are all sinners and God gets around to punishing some of us sooner than others.

Second, the answer must be one that can be given to the parents of a child who has died without rubbing salt in their wounds. "He's in a better place now," "At least you had him for X years," "Someday you will understand why this was the right thing to happen"—statements like these do not meet my standard.

Third, and similar to the second, it must be an answer that can be offered to survivors of the Holocaust without making them want to slap your face. I cringe at the words of some Orthodox rabbis who feel the need to justify God at the expense of the martyrs of Auschwitz and the Warsaw Ghetto, saying things like "It was God's punishment on Jews for forsaking the traditional ways." (But so many of the victims were pious Jews, and even if they weren't, is a firing squad or a gas chamber an appropriate punishment for working on the Sabbath?) Or they may say, "It was God's way of shaming the nations of the world into establishing the State of Israel," as if an omnipotent God could not find a less bloodthirsty way of bringing that about.

Almost seventy years after the end of World War II, it is hard to overestimate the impact of the Holocaust on people's ability to have faith in God and in God's world. I have had countless conversations with people who told me they no longer believe in God. I have debated the late Christopher Hitchens and other notables who publicly proclaim their atheism. I have spoken to a hundred or more adolescents who told me that they don't believe in God. Some of them come to that conclusion on philosophical grounds, some because they resent the idea of an authority telling them they can't do something they want to do. But in the overwhelming majority of cases, people have lost faith in God because of Hitler; because of atrocities in Cambodia, Rwanda, Sudan, and other countries; because of the untimely death of someone they loved; or because they look at the world, they listen to the news, and they cannot believe there is an all-powerful, benevolent deity in charge of things.

I recently read an excerpt from a sermon of Rabbi Kalman Kalonymous Shapira, leader of a small Hasidic community near Warsaw before the Second World War and later the much-beloved rabbi of the Warsaw Ghetto. The sermon was delivered in November 1939, shortly after the Nazis invaded Poland and began murdering Jews. Rabbi Shapira cites the familiar story found in Genesis 22 in which Abraham, as you will remember, is commanded to offer his son Isaac as a sacrifice, only to have the boy spared at the last moment. One can understand why that story would be on the minds of Polish Jews in November 1939. But Rabbi Shapira did not invoke the story to tell his congregation to have faith in God, who would intervene at the last moment to spare them. He connected the story to the first verse of chapter 23, which tells of the death of Abraham's wife, Sarah, and cited a well-known rabbinic tradition that Sarah died of shock and grief when she realized how close her son had come to dying. He then went on to address his sermon directly to God. In an act of astonishing boldness, he told God that Sarah's faith would ordinarily have been strong enough to survive that ordeal, but that she willed herself to die to warn God of the consequences of letting such things happen. If God did not stop the Nazis, many people's faith would not be up to that test, and they would abandon God and Judaism.

Alas, God did not heed Rabbi Shapira's warning. The angel did not intervene to spare the Jews of Poland, and for every Jew who lost his life in the Holocaust, there may now be hundreds of Jews and non-Jews who find it hard to believe in the goodness and power of God. If there is more interest in the book of Job today among people who are not regular students of the Bible, I think we can attribute that to two things: to cancer and to Adolf Hitler. It is hard to read of the Nazi treatment of Jews, Poles, gays, and other "inferior" people and still believe in God, unless, as C. S. Lewis warned us, tragedy leads people to conclude that God exists and He is a monster.

Finally, and personally, I deem unacceptable any explanation of God's role in our suffering that leaves people thinking less well of God than they did before. Statements like "There is a God but He is cruel, vain, and vindictive" or "There is a God but He doesn't care about us" would fall into that category.

How have people over the centuries tried to make sense of the book of Job, of Job's challenges, the consolations of his visitors, and God's answer out of the whirlwind?

Maimonides on Job

Moses Maimonides (1135–1204) was probably blessed with the greatest mind of any Jew between the death of the biblical Moses and the birth of Albert Einstein. At a relatively early age, he had not only mastered the entire Talmud, a lifetime project for most people, but reorganized it into an encyclopedic compendium in which anyone could find what Jewish law demanded of him without having to master Talmud himself. He did this so that Jews would not have to spend years studying Talmud but would be free to study philosophy and theology and come to better understand the true nature of God. To that end, he wrote his masterpiece, *The Guide for the Perplexed*, the first and probably still the foremost world-class theological work to come from Jewish sources. As we will see, this bias in favor of true knowledge of God over obedience to God's word will color Maimonides's understanding of the biblical book of Job.

In the process of writing a comprehensive book about God, Maimonides had to deal with the issue of good people suffering, and that meant trying to understand Job. He himself was no stranger to sorrow. His life changed dramatically for the worse when his beloved brother, a successful merchant who had been subsidizing Maimonides's life of study and writing, died in an accident at sea in which a ship laden with merchandise he was importing sank. Deprived of his brother's financial support, Maimonides had to work full-time as a physician; he studied, wrote his books, and answered his correspondence at night.

When he came to apply his formidable intellect to the book of Job, he labored under one insurmountable handicap that was not of his own making: He lived in the twelfth century. He had no alternative but to accept the traditional view of the book, that Job's problems were the result of God's wager with Satan, that the Fable and the Poem were of one piece by a single author, and that Elihu's intervention was part of the original book. In fact, since Elihu comes toward the end of the book, his views must be the (divinely inspired) author's final words on the subject. God's words from the whirlwind are an anticlimax.

Maimonides summarizes his understanding of the book early in his discussion of evil. Job, he writes, "is not said to be a wise or comprehending or intelligent person. Only moral virtue and righteousness are ascribed to him." In other words, Job was an incomplete person who thought that living righteously in accordance with the Torah was all that God expected of him. He had to undergo all those tribulations to attain a true knowledge of God (*Guide*, book 3, chap. 22, p. 487, in the Pines translation). Had Job possessed true insight into the nature of God, he would not have been spared illness and bereavement, but he would have understood them differently. He would have realized that true happiness is not a matter of health, wealth, and family but results from true knowledge of God. His friends likewise had a deficient understanding of God, thinking that Job's loss of health, wealth, and children was a tragedy. That is why God rebukes them at the end of the book for having spoken falsely of Him when they were under the impression that they had been defending God. God needs no defense; He is incapable of being unjust. To the conundrum of how evil can exist if God is all-good and all-powerful, Maimonides's answer is to affirm that suffering comes from God but to deny that it is evil. It is a necessary learning and growing experience.

Maimonides praises Elihu as "the most perfect among them in knowledge" (*Guide*, p. 494) and finds the key to understanding the book in Elihu's argument that sometimes people who have an oversimplified understanding of God require the experience of suffering to bring them to theological maturity. We recall that C. S. Lewis had a similar theory, pain as God's chisel to shape and perfect us, until reality compelled him to give it up. Maimonides, though he also suffered misfortune, resists the impact of reality. For him, what happened to Job (and to his own brother) was not evil. It may seem that way to us only because of our theological immaturity.

Does that mean that God is not committed to justice, to rewarding virtue and punishing vice? Can God be unjust? Is God permitted to do things that, had they been done by humans, would be crimes? One of Maimonides's major contributions to the challenge of speaking about God is his doctrine of "negative attributes." Because God is so radically different from human beings, some words, when applied to God, don't mean what they mean when applied to humans. We can only speak about God negatively, denoting what He is not. To say that God exists is not to make a statement about the existence of an actual being. It is to say that God is not imaginary. He is not nonexistent. To speak of God getting angry does not mean that He loses His temper the way we do. It means that He is not uncaring. All references to God's physical body are metaphors. If we speak of our deeds finding favor in the eyes of God, of our prayers reaching the ears of God, of the hand of God smiting the Egyptians, we are not saying that God is an actual person who lives in the sky and has eyes, ears, and hands. They are a poetic way of describing God's involvement in our lives. That works well enough when it comes to issues of God's corporeality. But what about such attributes as kindness, justice, and love? Maimonides would tell us that God is just, but not in the same way that earthly beings are just. God has His own notion of justice, and the death of Job's innocent children did not violate it. Scholars refer to that as "equivocal predication," using the same words we use for humans but with different connotations.

I find the doctrine of equivocal predication problematic. It makes meaningful theological conversation virtually impossible. Is God fair? Yes, but the word "fair" doesn't mean the same thing when we speak about God as it does when we apply it to people. Does God love me and care about my unhappiness? Yes, but not in the way that friends love you and care about you. Maimonides's explanation that God brought about the death of Job's children as part of an effort to bring Job to true knowledge of God fails on at least one of the criteria I set out earlier. It does not comfort the bereaved, and it may leave us thinking less well of God.

Leo Strauss, one of the foremost scholars of Maimonides in the twentieth century, offers the provocative theory, based on some tantalizing passages in Maimonides, that the *Guide* was not meant for the average reader but for the thoughtful specialist, and that there are esoteric messages hidden in the text that only a few true disciples would be able to understand. I don't find that a plausible or useful notion.

In the final analysis, despite my reluctance to dispute or criticize Maimonides, I find something fundamentally unsatisfying, even (dare I say it?) un-Jewish, about his position that a life based on piety and good deeds is religiously inferior to a life of theological speculation. It is a charge that will be made even more sharply by the next thinker we will consider.

Spinoza on Job

Benedict (Baruch) Spinoza (1632–1672) was a brilliant man obsessed with God and alienated by what was taught about God in his synagogue in Amsterdam. The one thing most Jews know about Spinoza is that he was excommunicated by the elders of the Amsterdam Jewish community for reasons never completely spelled out. Philosophy professor Rebecca Goldstein's biography of Spinoza for the Nextbook Jewish Encounters series puts forth the theory that Spinoza's quest to fashion a basis for belief in God and in religion on logical, virtually geometric principles was his response to what he saw in the Inquisition, where terrible things resulted from an excess of emotion in the name of religious loyalty.

Spinoza called the book of Job "the most honest book in the Bible" because it dared to question God's goodness and the extent of His involvement in human misfortune. He is unsparing in his criticism of Maimonides, accusing him of importing Hellenic categories of thought, derived from Aristotle, into the pages of the Hebrew Bible, elevating intellectual perfection over moral excellence. For him, the Bible is a guide to righteous living, not correct theological understanding.

Spinoza's own theory of Job is fairly unique, and is rooted in a comment by the twelfth-century Bible commentator Abraham ibn Ezra, who suggested that the book of Job was originally written in a language other than Hebrew. To this, Spinoza adds the observation that Ezekiel (14:14) refers to Job, along with Noah and Daniel (not the one from the lions' den), as examples of righteous gentiles. Aha, says, Spinoza, Job was written by a non-Jewish author presenting Job as a gentile role model, and that is why the God described in Job is so different from the God of the rest of the Bible. Job, he suggests, was included in the canon along with the equally non-Jewish book of Ecclesiastes, during late Second Temple times, when the authorities were open to gentile philosophy. I can appreciate why Spinoza would have been drawn to the radical theological honesty of the book of Job. It challenges the conventional Jewish understanding of God, just as he himself did. I can even understand, given his encounters with the rabbis of Amsterdam, why he might have doubted that a Jew could have written it. But I, living three hundred years later, find Job a thoroughly Jewish book, especially in its preference for truth and honesty over received doctrine.

The Kabbalah of Isaac Luria

Isaac Luria (1534–1572) was a sixteenth-century kabbalist and mystic, fashioner of one of the most provocative and influential kabbalistic theologies. Born in Jerusalem a century before Spinoza and schooled in Egypt, as a young man Luria settled in the Galilean city of Safed, then as now a center of mystical speculation. Though he never specifically deals with the book of Job, his theories lend themselves to a unique understanding of it.

Jewish mysticism tends to flourish in times of travail, when thoughtful people are moved to think there must be more to life than the sorrowful, blood-drenched world they see around them. There was a surge of mystical speculation in the years between the destruction of the Second Temple and the ill-fated Bar Kochba revolt in the second century of the Common Era, as captured in the story of Rabbi Akiva and the *pardes.* The Talmud describes how Akiva, the greatest scholar of his generation, and three distinguished colleagues joined in a mystical (possibly drug-aided) quest to penetrate the veneer of reality that separates us from understanding firsthand the secrets of the universe. Life was so unbearable under Roman domination that they felt this could not be the true world fashioned by God. One of the four lost his mind in the process, one lost his faith, one died; only Akiva emerged intact.

Kabbalah flourished in southern France in the wake of the destruction wrought by the Crusades. And it is plausible that Luria's theology, answering the question Why is the world such a mess?, was a reaction to the collapse of the once-great Jewish world of southern Spain.

Luria's narrative of the past, present, and future of God's world comes in three stages. The first is *tzimtzum*, God's contraction or withdrawal. In the beginning, God was everywhere, and all there was, was God. God then withdrew from one small corner of existence, leaving a space from which He would be absent, so that something other than God could exist. We can think of that as Creation Past.

In stage 2, God poured His creative energy into the space He had left vacant, to fashion a world. But the cleared space, devoid of God's presence, was too fragile to contain God's spirit and the vessels into which God had poured His spirit shattered under the strain. This is known in Lurianic kabbalah as *shevirat ha-kelim*, the shattering of the receptacles. As a result, the world God fashioned, the world we have come to live in, is a patchwork of incomplete fragments that were once touched by God. That would represent Creation Present, the current state of affairs.

The final stage, Creation Future, is called by a term that has become familiar in recent years, *tikkun olam*, repairing the world. *Tikkun olam* has become the slogan of countless idealistic Jewish youth groups, applied to efforts to feed the hungry and house the homeless. But in Luria's thought, it has a deeper theological meaning. It refers to the obligation of Jews to identify the shards of an imperfect world that still bear God's fingerprints and restore them to wholeness. Every ritual, every religious deed a Jew performs in the service of doing God's will puts one more piece of the puzzle in place until, one day, the world will be as perfect as God intended it to be. Seen from Luria's perspective, *tikkun olam* is not limited to acts of charity. Every act of self-restraint, every observance of the Jewish dietary laws, every moment of true intimacy between a husband and a wife, represents *tikkun olam*. Rather than asking, Why do these things happen?, Luria would have us focus on the question What can I do about them? When we do, we will find our answer not in theological speculation alone but in theological speculation that leads to life-sanctifying behavior by and between people. For the kabbalists, everything that exists is a fragment of those original shattered vessels. Everything is potentially holy, and our task in redeeming a broken world is to recognize and realize that potential holiness.

The kabbalah of Isaac Luria spoke to many Jews, for at least two reasons. First, it affirmed the omnipotence of God without holding Him directly accountable for the world's evil. The messiness of the world is due to human limitations, not divine ones. At most, God is responsible for overestimating the ability of the world to contain pure, undiluted divinity. Second and more important, it empowered the average Jew at a time when he was feeling most powerless. It said to him, You are not the helpless victim of Christian and Muslim malice. You are a soldier in the effort to redeem and restore the world. Every time you do something to call forth the hidden holiness of the ordinary moment, you help bring about the redemption.

What does all this have to do with the book of Job? Luria's theology makes it possible to reject the notion that Job's suffering was the will of God without having to compromise God's greatness and power. Suffering is part of the messiness of an unredeemed world, a world too fragile to contain God's pure holiness. What intrigues me about Lurianic kabbalah in relation to the question of Job is that it makes a crucial distinction between unfairness resulting from God's will and unfairness resulting from God's laws acting impersonally on innocent victims. God did not cause Job's afflictions: He created a world, the natural laws of which made them possible.

Martin Buber and the Hidden God

Martin Buber (1878–1965), theologian and chronicler of Hasidic tales, was born in Vienna and taught theology at the University of Frankfurt until the ascent of Nazism made his living and working in Germany untenable. He moved to Palestine (before it became Israel) in 1938. Inevitably, his views on God's involvement in our suffering, including a 1949 essay, "Job," in his book *The Prophetic Faith*, were colored by his encounter with and escape from Nazism.

At the heart of Buber's understanding of God's role in misfortune is a passage from the Torah, chapter 31 of Deuteronomy, in which God warns Moses that, after his death, "this people will go astray after the alien gods in their midst . . . Then My anger will flare up against them and I will abandon them and hide My countenance from them . . . and many evils and troubles shall befall them . . . Yet I will keep My countenance hidden on that day" (31:16–18).

Buber developed the concept of *hastarat panim*, God's hiding His face. Terrible things happen to people, not because God wills it but because God is upset with them and turns His attention from them, leaving them unprotected against the power of evil. God loves His people Israel but, from time to time, He is so dismayed by their misbehavior that He turns His face away.

In Buber's brief essay about Job in *The Prophetic Faith*, he describes Job's friends as defending "a reasonable and rational God, a God whom Job does not perceive either in our existence or in the world, a God who exists nowhere except in the domain of religion." The message he finds in the speech from the whirlwind is that God is just, but (and here we find an echo of Maimonides) His is not *compensatory justice*, righting wrongs and giving everyone what they deserve, but *distributive justice*, "bestowing on each creature what belongs to it." In the end, Job is capable of believing in justice despite his believing in an unjust God, and of believing in God in spite of believing in the necessity of justice, and resigns himself to living with the inconsistency.

I was never that impressed by Buber's concept of *hastarat panim*, the idea that misfortune comes when God has directed His attention away from us. To me, it seems not so much to explain Nazi cruelty as to explain God's failure to protect Jews from that cruelty. I always found that an unhelpful concept. I was inclined to see an autobiographical dimension to it, mindful of the fact that Buber's parents divorced when he was young and he was raised by his paternal grandfather, a Judaic scholar who turned young Martin into one. The doctrine of *hastarat panim* sounds a lot like the musing of a child of divorcing parents telling himself, "My father really loves me and wants to be with me, but I must have done something to make him leave me, and even though he would like to come back and be with me, sometimes he finds that impossible." But then I read Professor Jon Levenson's book *Creation and the Persistence of Evil*. Levenson is professor of religion at Harvard. The central thesis of his provocative and persuasive book is that the Bible's first words, describing God creating a world smoothly and effortlessly, turning chaos into order, are not the Bible's last words on the subject. Buried in the text and peeking through in passages from the Psalms and prophets are hints of another Creation story. In Genesis 1, God exercises complete, unchallenged mastery. The waters obey His command. The sea monster is just another one of His creatures. But in the counter-story, which Levenson calls the "combat theory" of Creation, paralleling similar accounts in other Near Eastern mythologies, it takes considerable effort for God to set limits to chaos and, at best, His victories are temporary. Levenson writes, "The absolute sovereignty of the God of Israel is not a simple given in the Hebrew Bible. . . . YHWH's mastery is often fragile, in constant need of reactivation and reassertion, and at times, as in the laments, painfully distant from our own experience. . . . Leviathan is still loose and the absolute sovereignty of God lies ahead."

Thus the Psalms frequently implore God:

Rouse Yourself, why do You sleep, O God?
Awaken, do not reject us forever.

Why do You hide Your face, ignoring our affliction and
distress? (Psalm 44:23–24)

Or in Psalm 74:

Till when, O God, will the foe blaspheme,
Will the enemy forever revile Your Name?
Why do You hold back Your right hand? (74:10–11)

At least one post-biblical commentator finds a hint of
this outlook in the book of Esther. As readers of that story
will recall, for the first half of the book, everything is working out according to the wicked Haman's plan. He has royal
permission to kill all the Jews of the Persian Empire. The
abrupt turning point of the story comes at the precise mid-
point of the book, where one would expect a skilled novelist
to place it, in a seemingly innocuous verse, Esther 6:1, "That
night, the king could not sleep." According to the Midrash
Rabbah to the book of Esther, "The reference is to the King
of Kings." How did the Jews of Persia come to find themselves at the mercy of a dreadful villain, leaving readers to
wonder, "Why is God letting this happen to His people?"
The commentator's answer would be that God's attention
was elsewhere. Only when things got desperate did the King
of Kings rouse Himself.

From this theological perspective, biblical Jews respond
to affliction not by asking, Why is this happening? or What
did we do to deserve this?, but by asking, Why doesn't God

do something about it? The God they believe in and rely on is *potentially omnipotent*. He could, if not destroy evil forever, temporarily defeat and confine it, as He did to that symbol of threatening chaos, the Sea.

Levenson goes on to write, "The possibility of an interruption in [God's] faithfulness is indeed troubling, [and] I find it especially odd that scholars who lived through the years of the Holocaust and other unspeakable horrors of our century should have imagined that the Hebrew Bible consistently upheld a doctrine of God's uniform, uninterrupted kingship, in spite of ample textual evidence to the contrary."

What are we to make of Levenson's reading of biblical theology, and what light does it shed on what Buber has to say on the subject? On the whole, I find Levenson persuasive. I am ready to believe that the Israelites saw misfortune as stemming from God's noninvolvement rather than from God's limitations or malevolence. But as a theology for today rather than an exercise in reading the Bible, I am not persuaded that what it takes to rouse God to confront evil is a Buberian reminder that there is a problem and would He please do something about it. God comes across as resembling the retired hero of a Western movie who can be prevailed upon to come to the rescue of the innocent by a combination of desperate pleas and flattery. I have no reason to believe that is how Levenson himself sees God; it is what he finds in Scripture. I am not sure about Buber.

Abraham Joshua Heschel and
the Pathos of God

A braham Joshua Heschel (1905–1972), who was my teacher, is probably best known to the American public for the iconic photo of his marching arm in arm with Martin Luther King Jr. in a civil rights protest in Selma, Alabama. Many a reporter at the scene noted that, with his luxuriant beard, he looked like an Old Testament prophet. That march and the friendship with King that developed from it were the culmination of a long process of personal growth for this scion of several of the great Hasidic dynasties of Jewish Poland, born into a world where suspicion of gentiles and gentile clergy was common. Though he was among the most prolific theologians of his generation, Heschel wrote very little specifically about Job. I was able to find only one brief treatment of the book of Job in his writings. It appears in his early work *God in Search of Man*, written when he was in his forties. In it, he assumes the unity of the book and sees Job's trials as a legitimate way for God to test whether any human being can be completely righteous without an element of self-interest. Heschel sees the book of Job less as a theodicy, a human effort to justify the goodness of God, and more as "anthropodicy, the justification of Man. . . . Is there anything pure and untinged with selfishness in the soul of Man? Is integrity at all possible?" The comment, with its hint that even good deeds may be contaminated by calculation or pride, seems flavored by Heschel's friendship with the Protestant theologian Reinhold Niebuhr, who held that view, and his appreciation of Niebuhr's thought.

But if he was not drawn to the book of Job, he was deeply concerned with the issue of good people suffering. How could he not have been, as he became aware of what the Nazis had done to the world of East European Jewry in which he had grown up, a world he eulogized memorably in his book *The Earth Is the Lord's*? Much of what I have to say about Heschel's theological understanding of God's role in our travail reflects what he wrote in his last book, his magnum opus, *Heavenly Torah as Refracted Through the Generations*, translated ably from the Hebrew by Rabbi Gordon Tucker, and draws on a perceptive article by Rabbi Geoffrey Claussen in the Summer 2010 issue of the magazine *Conservative Judaism*.

On the question of whether God is omnipotent and therefore responsible for all the calamities that befall good people, Claussen writes that "Heschel describes the school of Rabbi Akiva as [teaching] that God is not omnipotent. Faced with the reality of righteous people suffering, Akiva and his students refused to believe that God was unjust. Instead, they saw God as compassionate but limited in strength." In Heschel's own words, "Rabbi Akiva and his cohorts believed it is better to limit God's power than to dampen faith in God's mercy. . . . Between mercy and power, mercy takes precedence." And Heschel's own views tilt strongly in that direction. Claussen quotes from Heschel's earliest book, *Man Is*

Not Alone, to make the point that "viewing God as responsible for human suffering is a way of avoiding responsibility." And in an essay published posthumously, Heschel was even more explicit. "The idea of absolute omnipotence is somewhat missing in classical Jewish theology. This is really the impact of Islam. . . . Holding God responsible for everything, expecting Him to do the impossible, to defy human freedom, is a non-Jewish idea" (*Moral Grandeur*, p. 159).

What, then, is God's role when good people suffer? "The participation of the Holy One Blessed be He is that of total identification." When the Talmud describes the death by torture of Rabbi Akiva as *yissurin shel ahavah*, "chastisements of love," Heschel understands the phrase not as usually interpreted, to imply that God showed His love for Akiva by having him undergo the pain, like a parent punishing a wayward child ("this hurts me more than it hurts you") or a doctor operating on a patient. Rather, witnessing Akiva's martyrdom moves God to love him even more. The chastisements *create* a bond of love between God and the suffering victim, letting him know that he is not alone in his suffering.

For Heschel, some unmerited suffering (the result of a violent crime, theft, deceit) is caused by humans misusing their free will. But much is the result of "decrees [that] sometimes have unintended effects that cannot be taken back once they have the authority of the ruler behind them." A man leans too far out of a window and falls to his death, the result not of God's plan for him but of the law of gravity. A bridge spanning a river collapses at the height of rush hour because time and stress have taken their toll on the steel and concrete, as happened in Minnesota a few years ago, and dozens of innocent people perish. It was not God's will that those specific individuals die on that day, but it is God's will that the materials out of which the bridge was fashioned need constant maintenance to retain their strength.

Heschel was descended on his father's side from some of the greatest figures of early Hasidism, men who taught that God was present in everything that happened in the world, for good or ill. He was descended on his mother's side from Rabbi Levi Yitzhak of Berditchev, beloved for his compassion for all people at all times. I can imagine that Heschel grew up hearing two conflicting messages, one that the bad things that happened were God's chastisements sent to instruct and perfect us, and the other that God was too kind and loving a sovereign to want to hurt us, and that His role would be to comfort us. Trying to understand the persistence of unfairness in the world and whether there might have been a reason why the Jews of Eastern Europe suffered the fate they did under Hitler, one suspects that it was the Berditchev legacy, the Torah of compassion, that prevailed: "Between mercy and power, mercy takes precedence."

Other Perspectives

A surprising number of biblical scholars come to the end of Job and decide that the author's answer is that there is no answer. God's ways remain a mystery, beyond our understanding. Gordis writes, "Any view of the universe that fully explains it is, on that account, untrue. A mystery remains. . . . What cannot be comprehended by reason must be embraced in love." In a similar vein, Moshe Greenberg, a fine Bible scholar who contributed a theological introduction to the JPS translation of Job, writes, "How can piety nurtured in prosperity prove truly deep-rooted and not merely a spiritual adjunct of good fortune? . . . The book of Job tells how one man suddenly awakened to the anarchy rampant in the world, yet his attachment to God outlived the ruin of his tidy system." Arthur Peake, a British theologian and Bible scholar, writes similarly in his book *The Problem of Suffering in the Old Testament:* "To trust God when we understand Him would be but a sorry triumph for religion. To trust God when we have every reason for distrusting Him . . . is the supreme victory of religion." I find these all to be moving statements of personal faith, but it puts the burden of affirming the goodness of the world on Man. God repeatedly disappoints us, He causes or permits terrible things to happen, but we magnanimously forgive Him.

Pope, whose commentary on Job in the Anchor Bible series has been so helpful, concedes, "God's queries are ironical in the extreme, almost to the point of absurdity . . . The complete evasion of the issue as Job had posed it must be the poet's oblique way of admitting that there is no satisfactory answer available to man, apart from faith." I find it hard to believe that the genius who put so much imagination and effort into creating a masterpiece that would challenge the conventional theology of the Fable and engross scholars for millennia had in mind to end it with a shrug. With all due respect to Pope, who is a far better biblical scholar than I am, saying that one cannot find an answer in the speech from the whirlwind is not the same as saying that there is no answer there.

A second school of interpretation would tell us that there is an answer to be found in chapters 38–41, and the answer is "It's not all about you." God, in creating a world, filled it with all sorts of creatures, from ostriches to mosquitoes. He makes the rain fall and flowers grow in places inaccessible to humans, and it is not for us to ask him why. There is a passage in the book of Exodus (15:22–25), right after the Israelites cross the Red Sea, in which the people come to an oasis but find the water there polluted and undrinkable. God tells Moses to throw a branch from a certain tree into the water, and that will purify it. The rabbis in the midrash imagine a conversation between Moses and God in which Moses asks God, "Why did You create brackish water in Your world? It is of no use to anyone." God answers him, "It's not your job to understand. It's your job to do something to sweeten the water." If at times God's world causes us grief, from plagues killing thousands to snowstorms ravaging a city, that is a consequence, not a punishment. It was not done with us in mind. The task of religion is not to explain why the water is bitter or to justify its bitterness, but to sweeten it to slake our thirst, not to help us understand the cause of our misfortune but to help us cope with it (which is why I wrote a book called *When Bad Things Happen to Good People* rather than *Why Bad Things Happen . . .*).

Alter characterizes the Poem of Job as "a radical challenge to the doctrine of reward for the righteous and punishment for the wicked, [and] an equally radical rejection of the anthropocentric conception of Creation that is expressed in biblical texts from Genesis onward." Alter is right that every page of the Bible describes God as creating an entire universe but having a special relationship to the human beings in that universe, from creating the first humans in His image to intervening to bring the slaves out of Egypt, to entering into a covenant with those liberated slaves at Sinai, to sending His prophets to Israel to summon the people back to the right path. The Poem of Job may be a unique theological challenge to biblical faith (though not totally unique; there are passages in the prophets and Psalms that ask Job's question about why God lets the righteous suffer), but I don't find it a challenge to the notion of God's special concern for human beings. God may come down to tell Job that it's not all about him; He cares for eagles and hippopotamuses also. But we don't find God explaining to hippopotamuses why He bothered to create human beings. I can see the sages incorporating a book into the Bible that challenges conventional theology on issues of reward and punishment from within the framework of that theology. But I can't see them including a book that denies the essential premise of the rest of Scripture.

In addition, an interpretation of Job that teaches that God does not care about us violates the fourth and last of my conditions for a satisfactory solution: It leaves us thinking less of God than we did before. We could more easily accept the notion that God has His reasons for hurting us than that He really doesn't care.

Archibald MacLeish on Job

I remember the day my anger at God for making my child suffer began to diminish. It was in February 1967. Three months earlier, doctors had told us that our son's slow growth and loss of hair was the result of a rare disease that was untreatable, incurable, and would cause his death at a young age. I was shattered by the unfairness of it. Given the theological outlook I had been exposed to at that point, I could understand that God might have reason to punish me; I might have been the most observant Jew in our town, but I was not perfect. There must have been times when I fell short of being a perfect exemplar of Judaism or of pastoral compassion. But why would God punish an innocent child, or punish me by striking my innocent child? I had to ask myself if I could continue to believe in, let alone serve, such a God.

I did what many parents of afflicted children do. I sat down and read everything I could find about my son's malady, and then I read everything I could find about the illness and death of children. That brought me to the book of Job, and to Nahum Glatzer's compendium of scholarly essays on Job. They were learned and eloquent, but not terribly helpful until I came to the last essay, by Archibald MacLeish, poet and playwright and author of *J.B.*, the Job story in modern dress.

My wife and I had seen *J.B.* on Broadway some time before. We were impressed by MacLeish's elegant writing and by his pithy capturing of Job's lament:

> I heard upon his dry dungheap
> That man cry out who cannot sleep:
> "If God is God, He is not good;
> If God is good, He is not God."

That is the essence of Job's dilemma, isn't it? Do innocent people suffer because God does not care, in which case He is powerful but not good, or because He cares but can't do anything about it, in which case He is not God as we have been taught to imagine God?

J.B. is the story of a good man, a successful businessman and loving husband and father, who praises God for having blessed him with so much and implies that he must deserve it for being such a good person. He repays God with piety and praise. Then his world is (literally) destroyed. His children are killed one by one, each in a senseless tragedy. His wife loses her faith at that point, but J.B. insists, "God will not punish without cause. God is just. . . . We have no choice but to be guilty. God is unthinkable if we are innocent." (This is Job of the Fable speaking, not Job of the Poem.)

Finally, his city is destroyed by a nuclear blast, and he is left alone in the rubble. He wonders why God has done this to him, and as in the Bible, three visitors try to explain it. MacLeish is at his best caricaturing Job's comforters.

The first is a Marxist who explains that there was nothing personal about the disasters that befell J.B. It was his misfortune to be a capitalist at a time when history called for the overthrow of the ruling class by the proletariat.

The second is a psychiatrist who explains to J.B. that categories of good and evil don't really apply to people. People can't help doing the things they do. They are driven by hunger, lust, and selfishness, even if they try to disguise them with a veneer of virtue. "Self has no will," he tells J.B. "There is no guilt. We are victims of our guilt, not guilty," to which J.B. replies, "I'd rather suffer every unspeakable suffering God sends, knowing that it was I that earned the need to suffer, I that acted, I that chose, than wash my hands with yours in that defiling innocence." (I love that phrase "defiling innocence" to describe the attitude that you didn't do anything wrong because you couldn't help yourself.)

The final visitor is a clergyman who says to J.B., What was your sin? You were a human being, inevitably imperfect. It was nothing particular that you did wrong, but you are a descendant of Adam and Eve and an heir to the stain of Original Sin. J.B. replies to him, "Yours is the cruelest comfort of them all, making the Creator of the universe the Miscreator, a party to the crimes He punishes." How dare a righteous God create a flawed, imperfect creature and then punish him for not being perfect?

After those exchanges, God appears, unseen but heard, reciting lines from chapter 38 of the biblical book, "Where were you when I laid the foundations of the earth . . . ," and J.B. is cowed into saying, "I had heard of You by the hearing of the ear, but now my eye sees You, wherefore I abhor myself and repent."

At this point in the play, the actors who have spoken God's lines and Satan's stand aside to evaluate what they have seen happen. The actor representing God says in effect, I expected Job to throw the message in My face after what I had done to him, but he didn't. "He just sat there. *He forgave Me*, in spite of everything he had suffered. . . . Who is the judge here? Who plays the hero, God or him? Is God to be forgiven?" The Satan character responds, "Isn't He? Job was innocent, You remember." The implication would be that God is unfair and arbitrary and Job is the hero of the play (and the hero of the drama of human history), forgiving God's unfairness and pledging more allegiance to Him than His actions toward us deserve.

Though my wife and I enjoyed the play as a theatrical experience when we saw it, I was not impressed by its implicit theology. I found that it never transcended the conventional theology of the Fable, nor did it confront any of the questions that arise in the Poem.

Then, that winter morning some forty-odd years ago, I read a sermon MacLeish had given in his church in Farmington, Connecticut, as included in the Glatzer volume. In it, he explains what he was trying to say about God, Man, and suffering in his play. He defines the question this way: "How can we believe in our lives unless we can believe in God, and how can we believe in God unless we can believe in the justice of God, and how can we believe in the justice of God in a world in which the innocent perish in rash, meaningless massacres, and brutal and dishonest men foul all the lovely things?"

His answer: God needed Job's suffering. God needed to know that Job would love Him and be faithful to Him not only when things went well but even when things went horribly badly. I was troubled by that description of God, too similar to the insecure God of the Fable, but MacLeish went on to elaborate. In the key passage of the sermon, MacLeish writes, "Man depends on God for all things; God depends on Man for one. Without Man's love, God does not exist as God, only as Creator, *and love is the one thing that no one, not even God, can command.* . . . Acceptance of God's will is not enough. Love, love of life, love of the world, love of God, love in spite of everything is the only possible answer to the ancient human cry against injustice."

Reading MacLeish's sermon, I understood for the first time the closing lines of his play. J.B.'s wife, who left him when he would not condemn God for the death of their children, returns and says to him, "You wanted justice, and there was none, only love."

She goes on to say:

> The candles in churches are out [that is, there are no
> answers in theology],
> The lights have gone out in the sky [there are no
> answers in science].
> Blow on the coal of the heart and we'll see by and by.

She is saying, The answer to your question will not be an explanation making sense of what happened to us, because it *doesn't* make sense. It will be a response, a stubborn willingness to go on living in a world where children die and cities are bombed, a world we have learned we cannot count on, but we will go on living in it because, God help us, it is the only world we have. Her message calls to mind the teaching of Viktor Frankl in *Man's Search for Meaning*, to the effect that we cannot control what the world does to us, but we can always control how we choose to respond to what the world does to us.

Is it possible to write a version of Job in which Job is the hero and God is a secondary character? And will it still be a religious story if you do? I think it may be possible, though I don't think it is what the biblical author had in mind. To him, and to me, God is still the hero of the drama. (Of course, one has to dismiss the Fable-Prologue as the work of another author to be able to say that.) Answer-as-response may be more authentically religious than answer-as-explanation. As Professor Heschel told us in class, "The Bible is not Israel's theology; it is God's anthropology." That is, the Bible comes not to teach us who God is but to teach us who God wants us to be. And Christian theologian Stanley Hauerwas once said to me, "What we owe a mentally or physically disabled child is not to ask why God permits this, but to ask ourselves what kind of community we must be so that this child can live as full a life as possible." A religious response to tragedy need not be solely about God. It can be about how the sufferer responds, whether with acceptance, with rage, or with a new understanding of how life works. It can be about how others respond to his or her pain, with pious explanations or with hugs and shared tears.

What made reading MacLeish a transformative experience for me was not so much his calling on us to forgive God for the miseries of the world to show how much we love Him. I found that verging on the condescending. I can believe in a less-than-all-powerful God but not in an emotionally needy one. What excited me was MacLeish's challenging the idea of God's omnipotence. I had heard hints of this before, but from atheists, not from believers. Now, all of a sudden, it began to make sense. There are some things beyond God's control. Of the three articles of faith—God is all-powerful, God is all-good, evil is real—this was the first time I had come across a challenge to the idea that God was all-powerful. My theological training had consistently been along the lines of affirming God's omnipotence. "If you don't understand why God lets certain things happen, the limitation is probably with you, not with God. God has His reasons." And as we recall, Maimonides questioned the appropriateness of attaching human qualities like goodness to God and expecting Him to be good in the same way that human beings are good. In one paragraph, MacLeish challenged that. If the facts of life compel us to choose between an all-powerful God who is not good as we conventionally understand goodness, or a God who is awesomely powerful but not all-controlling and is entirely good, why have we been celebrating God's power at the expense of His goodness for so many centuries? Who taught us to worship power as the ultimate virtue? Better a limited God than a cruel, uncaring one.

Theologian David Ray Griffin once said to me, "I believe God is all-powerful but His power is not the power to control; it is the power to enable. God can't prevent some things from happening but He can enable us to cope with them." I told him, "That helps me understand why in so many religious traditions God is symbolized by fire. Fire is not a thing; it's not an object. It is a process, liberating the energy hidden in a piece of wood or a lump of coal and turning it into something useful. But while fire can be warm and life-sustaining, it can also be destructive, not because fire is evil but because fire follows laws of its own."

Finally, may I offer my own understanding of the book of Job. It has been informed but not shaped by MacLeish's sermon, by his notion of a God with limits to His power. I find that MacLeish's emphasis on human love and God's need for human forgiveness leaves me less admiring of God. I don't want to feel superior to God, and I can't imagine a coherent theology that would claim that.

I begin with the conviction that the book's answer must lie hidden in God's second speech from the whirlwind, the Behemoth and Leviathan passage, and in Job's final seven words. To have God appear and speak to Job is an invention so audacious that the author must have intended it to contain the solution to the issue the book has raised. The Behemoth and Leviathan verses can't be just a reiteration of chapter 38, "Where were you when I laid the earth's foundation?" and of Job's first apology. The second round must contain a message that goes beyond that. But what ideas is the author putting into God's mouth?

When I wrote *When Bad Things Happen to Good People* in 1981, I found the answer in God's struggle with Leviathan. I imagined God saying to Job, It is a challenge for Me to try to control Leviathan, the power of chaos and randomness. What makes you think you can do better? Many readers were comforted by the suggestion that what had happened to them was not God's doing, but many were troubled by the notion of a God who is not completely in control, and biblical scholars challenged my understanding of the Leviathan verses. One was kind enough to write in a review, "I think Kushner may be right about God, but he is wrong about the book of Job."

Today, more than thirty years later, my understanding of Job and my understanding of God's role in our suffering have evolved. I am not sure I would still speak of God as limited; I can see where, for many readers, that would diminish God in their eyes, violating one of my criteria for an acceptable solution to Job's problems. Rather, I would speak of Him as self-limiting, along the lines of Luria's *tzimtzum*, God withdrawing from some area of existence to leave room for humans to be human. In the beginning, there was only God, and He was in total control. "Let there be . . . ," and there was. Then, as I understand it, God designated two areas of creation over which He would cede control. One was the domain of Nature and natural law. God is moral. He can tell the difference between a good person and a bad one. But Nature, as I said earlier, recognizes no obligation to be fair, inflicting drought on parts of the earth that thirst for rain and sending floods to places that crave sunshine. Nature blesses the undeserving with good looks, superior intelligence, and athletic skills that the rest of us can only envy. That is Leviathan, the agent of chaos and chance, at work. When I spoke in a New Orleans house of worship on the first anniversary of Hurricane Katrina, I told those in attendance, "You want to know why something like this could happen to you. I can give you the answer in six words: God is moral, Nature is not." I read to them the biblical passage from chapter 19 of the first book of Kings, Elijah on Mount Sinai. There we read, "There was a great and mighty wind, splitting mountains and shattering rocks . . . but the Lord was not in the wind. After the wind, an earthquake, but the Lord was not in the earthquake. After the earthquake, a fire, but the Lord was not in the fire. And after the fire, a still, small voice" (I Kings 19:11–12). I told the people of New Orleans, "The hurricane was not God; it was Nature, blind, uncaring Nature. The flood was not God. Where was God when your city was struck? His was the still, small voice moving some residents to go out in their rowboats and rescue you from your rooftops. His was the voice that inspired hundreds of college students to spend their spring break mopping the streets of New Orleans instead of partying on a beach in Fort Lauderdale. If they were not responding to a still, small voice from God, why did they do it?"

The sages in the Talmud use the expression *olam k'minhago noheg*, "the natural world follows its own laws" (Tractate Avodah Zarah 54b). For example, if a man steals seeds and plants them, justice would require that those seeds not germinate and the thief not profit from his crime. But Nature is not just, and stolen seeds grow as readily as honestly obtained ones. Falling rocks and speeding bullets obey the laws of Nature, not the preferences of God. They do their damage to whoever is in their path without considering whether he deserves to be injured or not. Natural disasters that destroy entire cities, malignant tumors that cut short a precious life, are the result of God not intervening to compel Nature to make exceptions for nice people.

The second area that God decreed off limits to His intervention is the human freedom to choose between good and evil, the challenge to tame Behemoth and put his immense energy to good use. If we were not free to reject good and prefer evil, our choice of goodness would be no more of a moral act than the sun's "choosing" to rise each morning in the east.

As I have now come to understand it, the book of Job celebrates God's awesome power but recognizes self-imposed limits on that power, to avoid compromising God's primary quality, His goodness. I hear God saying to Job, Behemoth and Leviathan, the Life Force and the element of Chaos, often mess up My world, but I need them. I could have created a perfect world, a clockwork world in which nothing regrettable would ever happen. In fact, such a world may have existed at some point in the distant past, but it lacked goodness, it lacked change, it lacked surprise, and I let it disappear. It was like seeing the same movie night after night. I chose instead to make a world of challenge and response, a world in which humans would eat the fruit of the Tree of Knowledge of Good and Evil and have to make a hundred decisions every day as to what was the right thing to do, learning from their mistakes when they got something wrong. It would be a world with no shortage of problems, but a world blessed with great minds and great souls to solve those problems, to invent things, to discover cures, to create great works of art that can only be born out of great pain (like the book of Job). And most important, I did not abandon this world when I finished making it. I was always here, comforting, inspiring, strengthening. Where do you think people would get the strength to overcome sorrow, to fight injustice, to heal the wounds of body and soul if I were not there to infuse some of My spirit into them? Your friends Eliphaz, Bildad, Zophar—they said some foolish things when they tried to comfort you, some hurtful things. But can you understand how hard it was for them to come and see you like this? Can you appreciate how much they hurt for you and wanted to make you feel better, even if they didn't have the right words? Their caring for you should balance the shallowness of their arguments.

Were there reasons for the terrible things that happened to you and your family? Yes, there were, but not the sort of reasons you were looking for. Your cattle were stolen not to punish you but because the Sabeans chose a life of crime and violence and I couldn't stop them without diminishing their humanity. Your children died not because they deserved to die but because Nature is blind and natural disasters are equal-opportunity destroyers.

And Job is satisfied, not so much by the content of God's answer as by the contact with God. You may remember the parable I cited earlier, about how Abraham came to believe in God. He was walking in the wilderness when he saw a palace "lit up by fire." Abraham mused to himself, *Does someone live in that palace?* God then appeared and said, "I am the Lord of this palace." As I said earlier, some have understood that story to mean that the lights were on, indicating that the palace was inhabited. There was a power in charge of the world. The beauty and order of the world, the human capacity for charity and goodness testify to the existence of God. And for years, that is how I understood the parable. I am now inclined toward those who take the words "lit up by fire" to mean that the palace was burning. Abraham thought, *What a shame! Such a lovely palace. Is it possible that no one lives there to care for it?* God then appeared and assured him, Don't worry. I am the Lord of this palace. It has not been abandoned.

The events of my personal and professional life have moved me over the years to accept that second reading of the story. I now find God not in the perfection of the world, the intricacies of rain and sun, growth and healing, the change of seasons and the beauty of the leaves in autumn. I find God in the miracle of human resilience in the face of the world's imperfections, even the world's cruelty. How are people able to survive tragedy (and that is what you do with tragedy: you don't understand or explain it, you survive it)? What gave survivors of the Holocaust the courage to remarry and create new families after what the Nazis and their collaborators did to their first families? What enabled our fourteen-year-old son, so stricken with congestive heart failure that he had to sleep standing up, to look forward to every day he had to share with his friends, his family, and his dog? What motivates doctors to search for cures, and neighbors to hug us and dry our tears when we are stricken, if it is not God at work within them and within us?

I find my own answer to Job's question, both a personal response and a theological answer, in Job's last seven words. Like Job, I have met God. I have met Him in the sunshine but more often in the shadows, not in the elegant perfection of the world but in the resilience of the human soul, the ability of people to find even a pain-filled life, even a grossly unfair life, worth living. I have met God in the readiness of people to reach out to the afflicted, to salve their wounds not with their doctrines but with their hugs and their tears. Like Job, like Abraham, I have seen a world in flames and I have been sustained by the message that God has not abandoned His world.

Having heard God say to Job, It will not be a perfect world, but it will be a world marked by great natural beauty, inspiring human creativity, and astonishing human resilience, and I will be with you in all of those times, I, like Job, respond:

Em'as v'nihamti al afar v'efer. I repudiate my past accusations, my doubts, even my anger. I have experienced the reality of God. I know that I am not alone, and, vulnerable mortal that I am, I am comforted.

ABOUT THE AUTHOR

Harold S. Kushner is rabbi laureate of Temple Israel in the Boston suburb of Natick, Massachusetts. A native of Brooklyn, New York, he is the author of nine best-selling books on coping with life's challenges and two volumes of collected sermons.